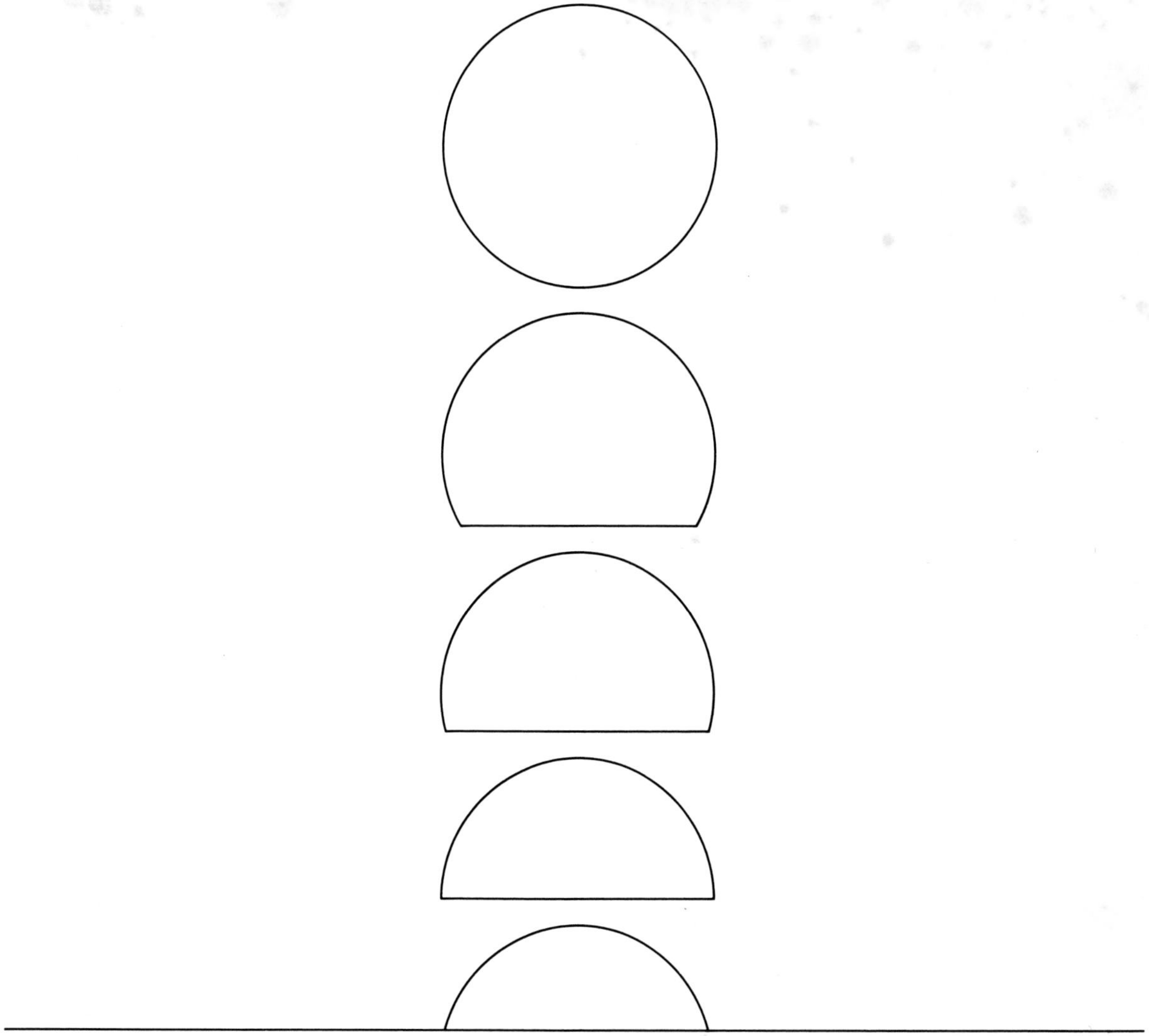

Robes of White Shell and Sunrise

6 This Lodge Maker's costume, worn on the fourth day of the Arapaho Sun Dance, exemplifies the ceremonial use of body painting. The design represents the setting sun. Arapaho, Wyoming and Oklahoma.

Robes of White Shell and Sunrise

Personal Decorative Arts of the Native American

by Richard Conn

Denver Art Museum

November 9, 1974-January 19, 1975

This book and the exhibition it accompanies have been made possible by the generous assistance and support of the Phillips Petroleum Company.

Library of Congress Catalog Card Number 74-16739
ISBN 0-914738-04-6
Printed in the United States of America

Denver Art Museum
100 West 14th Avenue Parkway
Denver, Colorado 80204

Cover detail: Yurok leather skirt decorated with shells and trade beads (cat. #92)
Photo by Lyle Don Carlos

Lenders to the Exhibition

The Anschutz Collection
Denver, Colorado

Mr. and Mrs. L. D. Bax
Denver, Colorado

Eastern Washington State Historical Society
Spokane, Washington

Field Museum of Natural History
Department of Anthropology
Chicago, Illinois

Robert H. Lowie Museum of Anthropology
University of California, Berkeley

Manitoba Museum of Man and Nature
Winnipeg, Manitoba

Milwaukee Public Museum
Milwaukee, Wisconsin

Montreal Museum of Fine Arts
Montreal, Quebec

National Museum of Man
Division of Ethnology
Ottawa, Ontario

University of Colorado Museum
Boulder, Colorado

Contents

We welcome the opportunity provided by the Denver Art Museum to help make possible this distinguished exhibition of a significant and remarkable part of the American heritage.

In these days when we salute the 200th anniversary of so many developments which led to the formation of the United States of America, it is fitting that we also recognize the personal decorative arts of the Native Americans who lived on this continent long before explorers came from across the seas.

Phillips Petroleum Company

Foreword

The Denver Art Museum is proud to present the first major exhibition devoted to the creativity of design found in the costume and personal decoration of the American Indian. In recent years public interest, nationally and even internationally, has focused increasingly upon Indian arts, life, and culture. Major exhibitions, such as those presented by New York's Whitney Museum in 1971 and by the Walker Art Center in Minneapolis in 1972, have been important milestones in the development of public appreciation for Native American esthetic achievements.

Since its earliest days, the Denver Art Museum and its supporters have been among the most active in encouraging broad interest and understanding of Indian art and culture through acquisitions, exhibitions, and publications. As a result, Indian art dominates the collections of the museum with approximately half of our 20,000 objects in that area. Works range from the lofty totem poles of the Northwest Coast to miniature Pomo baskets of intimate beauty and from subtly modeled Eskimo masks to expressive Iroquois sculpture.

Robes of White Shell and Sunrise is devoted to an area of particular strength in our collection, American Indian costume. The exhibition, one of the most ambitious and extensive ever undertaken by the museum in the field of Indian art, seeks to reveal the extraordinary richness and remarkable diversity of Indian design concepts. Also apparent are the sophisticated innovations of costume design and especially the complex social and religious symbolism inherent in costume decoration. It should be noted that selections of Indian jewelry are intentionally limited since the field is one the museum plans to explore in depth in a future exhibition.

On behalf of the trustees and staff of the museum, I wish to offer our profound appreciation to the Phillips Petroleum Company of Bartlesville, Oklahoma, which has generously underwritten the costs of the exhibition and its catalog. Our particular thanks go to W. F. Martin, Chairman of the Board and Chief Executive Officer, Wm. C. Douce, President, and Sloan K. Childers, Vice President Public Affairs, whose perception and support have permitted the realization of a significant exhibition of the artistic achievements of the Native American. In addition to financial support, they have provided the assistance of key members of their staff, to whom we are also grateful.

We are deeply indebted to the public and private collectors of the United States and Canada, whose names are recorded elsewhere, who have generously consented to lend important works to the exhibition. While it is a point of pride that the Denver Art Museum has been able to provide the majority of works on display, the success of the exhibition has been assured by the support of these lenders.

No one has been more central to the accomplishment of the entire task than Richard Conn, Curator of Native Arts. He has conceived and organized the exhibition, written its catalog, enlisted the valuable assistance of many volunteers, and in myriad ways brought the project to fruition.

Thomas N. Maytham
Director

Acknowledgments

An exhibition of this magnitude is not brought to public view without the dedicated cooperation and support of many institutions and individuals. The catalog and the exhibition have been made possible by a grant from the Phillips Petroleum Company, which also offered extensive technical assistance. It has been our pleasure to work with Sloan K. Childers, Vice President Public Affairs, and James Lynn, Public Relations Officer. Phillips' Creative Art Director, Lyle Don Carlos, proved an indispensable design consultant. His versatile talent and expertise are reflected in many facets of the undertaking.

To those who helped to provide important loans to complete our survey of Native American clothing, we extend sincere thanks. We are indebted to L. D. Bax of Denver, who graciously agreed to lend many fine pieces from his collection. For their ready encouragement and cooperation, we are particularly grateful to Denis Alsford, Curator of Collections of the National Museum of Man of Canada, Dr. David Hemphill, Director of the Manitoba Museum of Man and Nature, Dr. James A. Nason, Chairman of Anthropology at the Thomas Burke Memorial Washington State Museum, and Dr. Frank Norick, Senior Anthropologist at the Robert H. Lowie Museum of Anthropology at the University of California, Berkeley. The unique contribution of Philip F. Anschutz deserves special recognition. His enthusiasm and acumen were vital to the realization of the exhibition.

Those who modeled the garments illustrated here have helped breathe life into our understanding of Native American esthetics: Camille Clairmont, Jeffery Crabtree, John Haberman, Pershing High Hawk, Karl Johnson, Jolynne Locust, Vivian Locust, Dusty Nelson, Richard Peters, Kenneth Shelton, Mrs. Rodman L. Tidrick, Doris White Bull, and Michael Wolf. The talents of the museum staff have again been tapped to make the project a success. Marlene Chambers, editor of publications, devoted many hours to the design and layout of the catalog and proved invaluable in editing the text. The cheerful assistance of Phoebe Phillips, secretary, was indispensable to the preparation of the manuscript. The museum photographer, Lloyd Rule, worked tirelessly to achieve outstanding photographs for the catalog and assisted in the preparation of pictorial material for the exhibition. Publicity was provided by Linda Anderson, director of that department. Our special thanks go to Jeremy Hillhouse, exhibition designer, and to the production staff who aided in the installation of the exhibition.

So many museum volunteers contributed to the exhibition that it is difficult to single out any for special recognition. We were fortunate to have the assistance of Mrs. Charles Fisk and Mrs. F. M. Sassé, who were responsible for the restoration and preparation of materials for exhibition. Mrs. Robert D. Houston and Mrs. George L. Bethune worked diligently in preparing the exhibition itself. As in all the museum's undertakings, volunteer time has been of inestimable value.

An important benefit of our association with Phillips has been the creation of two temporary museum internships for Native American students at local universities. These positions have been awarded to Vivian Locust and Michael Wolf, South Dakota Sioux, who have participated in the installation and interpretation of the exhibition. It has been a mutually rewarding experience to work closely with them to create an exhibition that will allow our viewers to experience fully the significance of Native American art.

Richard Conn
Curator of Native Arts

The title of this catalog and the exhibition it accompanies has been inspired by a ceremonial prayer of the Zuni people, offered for blessing a novice upon his initiation into the Great Fire Society. We thank the Zuni for the use of this beautiful prayer, part of which is quoted here:

> Then when my fathers took hold of their
> prayer meal,
> Their shells,
> Their rich clothing,
> We of the daylight
> With the prayer meal,
> With the shells,
> With the rich clothing,
> We held one another fast.

As published in "Zuni Ritual Poetry" by Ruth L. Bunzel, *47th Annual Report of the Bureau of American Ethnology* (Washington, D.C., 1932), pp. 611-836.

American Indian Tribes

1 Acoma
2 Alaskan Eskimo
3 Aleut
4 Algonquin
5 Arapaho
6 Arikara
7 Assiniboine
8 Athabascan
9 Bella Coola
10 Beothuk
11 Blackfeet
12 Blood
13 Caribou Eskimo
14 Cheyenne
15 Chilcat
16 Chiricahua Apache
17 Coast Salish
18 Coeur d'Alene
19 Comanche
20 Copper Eskimo
21 Cowichan
22 Cree
23 Creek
24 Crow
25 Delaware
26 Gros Ventre
27 Haida
28 Hopi
29 Hupa
30 Huron
31 Iowa
32 Iroquois
33 Jemez
34 Jicarilla Apache
35 Karok
36 Kickapoo
37 Kiowa
38 Kutchin
39 Kwakiutl
40 Mackenzie Eskimo
41 Maidu
42 Mandan
43 Maricopa
44 Mescalero Apache
45 Menomini
46 Metis
47 Miami
48 Mojave
49 Nambe
50 Naskapi
51 Navajo
52 Nez Percé
53 Nootka
53 Ojibwa
55 Okanogan
56 Osage
57 Oto
58 Ottawa
59 Paiute
60 Pawnee
61 Pomo
62 Ponca
63 Potawatomi
64 San Juan
65 Santa Clara
66 Santee
67 Santo Domingo
68 Sarsi
69 Seminole
70 Seneca
71 Shoshone
72 Sioux
73 Spokane
74 Taos
75 Tanaina
76 Thompson River Salish
77 Tlingit
78 Tsimshian
79 Ute
80 Winnebago
81 Yuma
82 Yurok
83 Zuni

2
2
8
8
2
40
3
75
38
20
3
8
15
13
77
50
78
10
27
22
39
9
68
76
22
53
54
17
12
21
46
4
11
73
30
55
18
54
42
58
7
52
66
70
6
26
45
32
62
63
36
80
72
24
31
82
60
25
35
71
29
47
61
5
14
57
59
79
41
37
56
34
51
48
74
28
49
64
81
83
33
65
23
1
67
43
19
16
69
44

33, 74, 166 A wraparound skirt is featured in this purely decorative costume. Menomini, Wisconsin.

Instead of a Stereotype

This third quarter of the 20th century has been called by such qualifying epithets as the "Age of Anxiety." As a nation and as individuals, we seem to be reevaluating every aspect of our lives — our ideas, institutions, and even our material possessions — as if we were deciding what we now have that is worthy to be taken along into the next millennium. Among the excess baggage we might well discard are the many stereotyped images that have cluttered our minds. Some of these have already been jettisoned: few believe today, for instance, that tomatoes are poisonous or that all Norwegians are blondes. Certainly, the Native Americans — the many Indian groups and the Eskimos — have been the object of an incredible amount of this mental pigeon-holing. "All Indians live in wigwams and carve totem poles" runs the old saw, a patently ridiculous contradiction. This catalog and the exhibition it accompanies are devoted to the reexamination of one of the Native American's most attractive accomplishments, one particularly susceptible to stereotyping — his clothing. Although any thoughtful person will realize that our native people must have worn something more than blankets and feathered headdresses, movie and television screens continue to reinforce such false impressions by presenting hordes of ludicrously dressed "Indians." Old chestnuts are the hardest to crack!

At the same time, we are also experiencing today a resurgence of interest in Native American arts. Jewelry, textiles, sculpture, and other aspects of this broad field have been the subject of great exhibitions, many recent books, and much collecting activity. It is timely, then, to consider again the indigenous art manifested in covering and decorating one's person, especially since the native people themselves took these art forms seriously. The Indian saw his clothing as more than an object of practical utility. He viewed it as an important field for self-expression and esthetic activity. Imaginative clothing design could improve or modify his physical appearance and — in the case of certain ceremonial dress — turn him into another being altogether. The natural environment offered a plethora of materials for construction and decoration. Numerous possibilities for color and texture were available, as well as decorative materials capable of producing interesting sounds as the wearer moved about.

However, the Native American's clothing often served needs beyond those of basic protection and adornment. By its design and ornamentation a garment could reveal its owner's political rank or social status. In some tribal groups, certain clothing decorations were used to indicate the wearer's honored position within his family, his military prowess, his good deeds, or his membership in some special group. And, in a continent where religion tended to be a matter of individual expression, certain garments and accessories held complex sacred meaning.

Perhaps it was because the Native American did take his clothing seriously and because he used it as a symbolic means of communication that he created such striking and varied costumes. In many instances, dress and personal decoration are successfully realized attempts to inspire religious awe, frighten an enemy, or command attention and admiration. These ensembles are especially noteworthy for the creativity and originality they show. It may be justly said that the Native American has been the world's most interestingly dressed human being.

Let us abandon our stereotypes and actively begin to look once more. For the old stereotypes, let's substitute stereoscopy—another Greek-derived word which means "solid vision." If we will reexamine the personal decorative art of Native America with a vision solidly based upon a clear appreciation of its remarkable qualities, our enlarged understanding of its significance and beauty can do much to enrich our own lives.

Body DECORATION

Body Decoration

1

Most of the world's peoples seem to feel a periodic compulsion to transform their appearance — sometimes by a change of clothing, but more frequently by modifications to the body itself. Often these alterations are temporary, but others remain until the grave — and even longer. Men and women have sought for centuries to change their bodies into whatever was currently thought proper or attractive: by pinching in or padding out, by carving into living flesh or eliminating unwanted appendages, by removing or reshaping teeth, and even by modifying the bones themselves. Although the Native Americans did not practice grim varieties of self-improvement, they universally practiced body painting to serve a multitude of specific purposes.

The simplest kind of personal painting was functional, providing protection against unfavorable climate. People living in areas of high winds, bright sun, or temperature extremes sometimes painted themselves with transparent oil or animal grease to guard against these adverse conditions. The northern Plains people added ground red pigment to the grease as a protection against windburn. Similarly, some Northwest Coast tribes mixed pulverized fungus with hemlock gum as a safeguard against sunburn. Confronted with bright sun on deep snow, the native people of interior Alaska are said to have smeared a mixture of grease and powdered charcoal beneath their eyes to reduce glare. The Mojave and their neighbors on the lower Colorado River who experienced the discomfort of extreme midsummer heat even painted their long hair with mud and tied it into a tuft on top of their heads.

Most face and body paintings were, however, meant to accomplish something more than physical protection. Some were purely decorative, and others functioned in relation to some aspect of the wearer's culture: his religion, his personal accomplishments, or the social order and his place in it.

One might list hundreds of examples of paintings intended to do no more than create an attractive impression. For example, the Plains tribes who favored smooth hairdresses with neatly set single or multiple hair partings emphasized the precision of their coiffures by painting narrow red lines along the parting (cat. #1). Women sometimes added a small semicircle on the forehead, using originally a native red ocher ground in grease or water and later a more brilliant Chinese vermillion (powdered mercuric sulfide) that became available with the advent of the European trader. Participants in social dances over most of North America still paint their faces as fashion and imagination suggest.

A considerable number of face and body paintings originated in religious experience and were intended to confer special powers on their wearers. Occasionally such a design, in complete and intricate detail, was received by the fasting and praying supplicant in a direct vision. The pious postulant who faithfully performed appropriate religious exercises could hope to attract a guardian spirit who would teach him special prayers and songs, offer instructions for attaining some goal, and present visible proof of supernatural blessing, which often included directions for a magical face painting design. The painting itself, if correctly applied, was believed to possess an intrinsic sacred power that could, for example, render a warrior invulnerable in battle or help a woman cure the sick. Obviously, a design of this kind could work as an effective charm only for the individual who had dreamed it.

Other paintings belong to particular religious ceremonies and can only be worn by individuals while actively performing specified roles in the ritual. For the Sun Dance, the most sacred ceremony of the Arapaho people, the principal celebrant wears different costumes and body paintings each day of the rite. Every element of these paintings contributes to the symbolic meaning of the whole ceremony, which celebrates both the manifold beauties of the world and the gifts of life bestowed upon mankind by the Supreme Powers. On the fourth day, for example, the Lodge Maker's face is painted to represent the life-giving sun setting over the grassy earth (cat. #6). Several diamond-shaped figures signify the "eyes of the sun," and the black lines connecting them denote the sun's rays. Complex symbolic decorations like this may have originated in the dream of an individual and their intrinsic sacred power later incorporated into the fixed insignia of a specific ceremonial functionary.

Body painting has sometimes served as an easily identifiable badge of social rank. Among the people of the Northwest Coast, who lived in an atmosphere highly charged with social competitiveness, each clan (and within the clan, each family lineage) stretched the limits of its resources and the bounds of local etiquette as far as possible in attempts to gain increased prestige. On every appropriate occasion members of competing clans painted their faces with designs that proclaimed familial affiliations in terms calculated to remind others of the family's long and distinguished history. Since the Northwest Coast people had a well-developed iconography for the creatures of their heraldic art, it was essential that each animal figure or the abstraction based on it be correctly drawn. Accordingly, carved wooden stamps were used for applying precise face designs that would leave no room for mistaken identification.

Europeans have quite naturally failed to "read" body painting signs correctly. At one time, a painted Indian face meant only one thing to an outsider — aggression. Actually, "war paint" was usually not a declaration of belligerency but a magic protective device. The Mojave and their neighbors are an exception to the rule. Before attacking, these warriors painted their faces completely black to indicate their hostile intentions and to identify themselves to one another. Mojave war painting thus became part of a "team uniform." On the other hand, young Mandan warriors blackened their faces as they returned home with the first enemy scalps. Like a good many other Native American groups, the Mandans used "after-the-battle" face and body paintings to advertise their military exploits. In some cases, even women wore painted signs that allowed them to bask in the reflected glory of their husbands' brave deeds.

The art of face and body painting has been practiced for a good many other motives. In some tribes symbolic face paintings were used to designate such temporary states as mourning, marriage, or new paternity. Some peoples created special face painting to mark twins, who were considered a gift from heaven. The Beothuk tribe of Newfoundland, who were called the "Red Indians" by neighboring tribes and later by Europeans because they received a bath of red dye at semi-annual ceremonies, offer a unique instance of an entire community's being marked to strengthen their sense of tribal cohesiveness and identity.

Because painting produces only temporary alterations, it is a particularly appropriate method for creating purely decorative effects or signifying temporary conditions. Since tattooing marks one permanently, however, it was rarely used by the Native American solely for decoration. Indeed, tattooing was far less generally employed for any reason in America than it was in Africa or the South Pacific. Among Eskimo women, however, tattooing the face for decorative effect was once a common practice (cat. #9), and the Yuman-speaking peoples of southeastern California and adjacent Arizona tattooed both boys and girls at puberty in the belief that those without tattoos could not enter the afterworld.

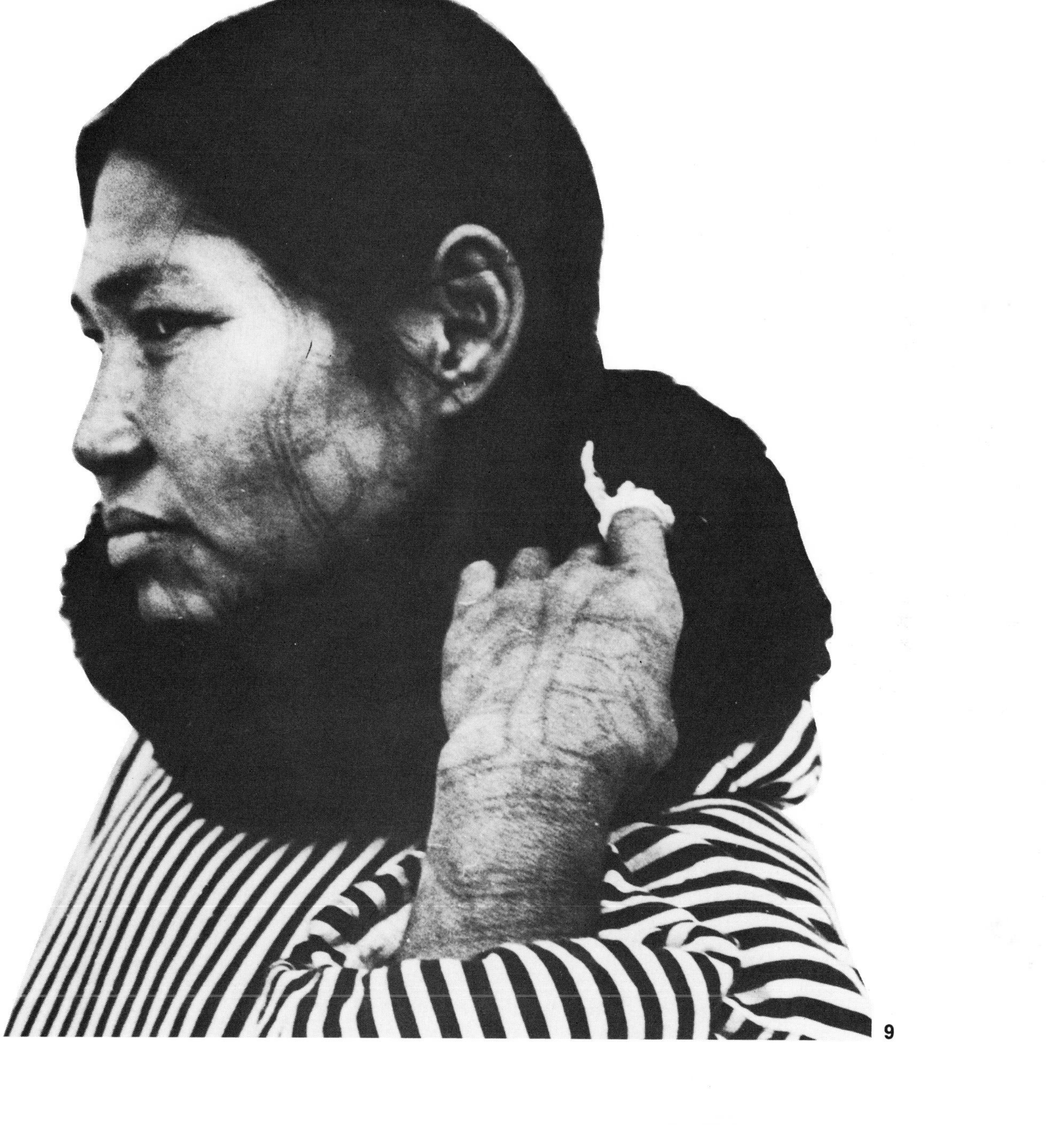

9

10

Another remarkable example of tattooing comes from the opposite corner of California. The native peoples of this area — such as the Yurok, Hupa, and Karok — had a concept of money much like our own. Their medium of exchange was the marine shell *Dentalium pretiosum,* and its value was determined by its length. Adult men of these tribes tattooed gauge lines on their forearms for ease in evaluating their seashells.

Tattooing was used most often in Native America, as in Africa and Polynesia, to proclaim social status. In certain groups, a tattooed face or body were the prerogatives of the local elite. The earliest example known to us from the New World was recorded by Jacques Le Moyne in Eastern Florida in 1564, when the French naval officer René de Laudonnière was received by Saturiba, the local chief. Le Moyne's only surviving sketch shows this noble gentleman tattooed from head to foot with designs that proclaimed his sovereignty. When the report of this voyage was published, Le Moyne's sketches were rendered as engravings (cat. #10) by Theodore de Bry of Frankfurt-am-Main. Among Northwest Coast peoples, persons of rank sometimes tattooed themselves with the heraldic animal figures that represented their clans and families. A young Haida man is illustrated here (cat. #11) with designs on his chest that refer to the bear and others on his forearms depicting eagles.

The Native American's custom of body painting and tattooing may have seemed exotic to European eyes, but his practice of head deformation appeared inhumane and even cruel. Since head deformation must be accomplished in infancy, Europeans felt certain the process inflicted unnecessary pain and permanently affected the child's intelligence. Today, of course, we know that head deformation actually caused no ill-effects. The binding pads or wrappers that touched the skull were always of the softest available materials, and the binding frames

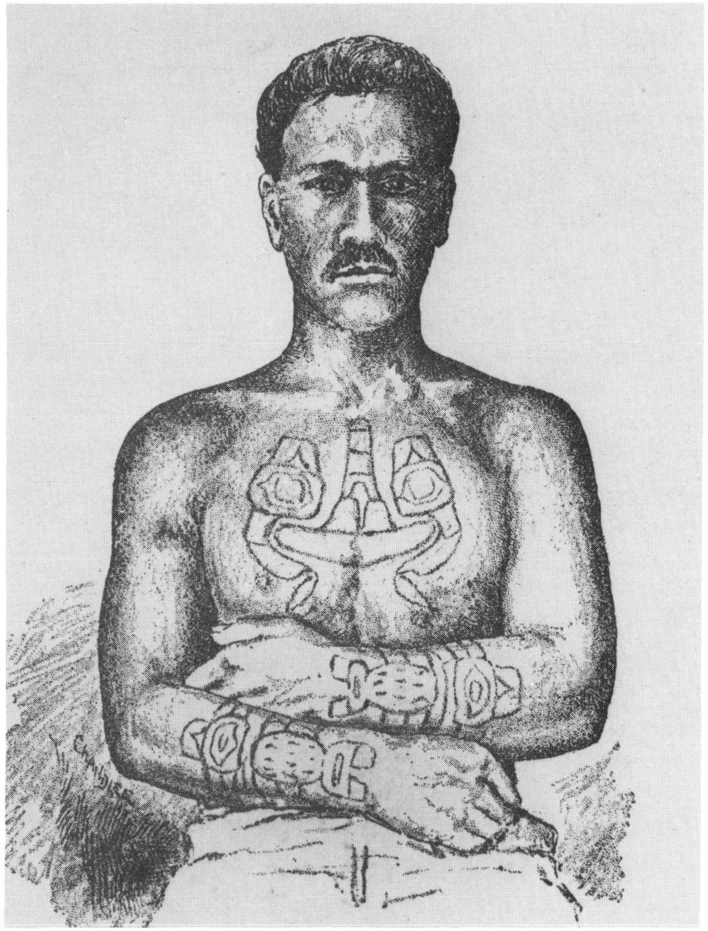

11

did not compress the skull (which would have been most painful) but merely changed its shape. In parts of Africa where head deformation is still practiced, examinations have shown that persons with modified skulls are as intelligent as their round-headed contemporaries. Although the custom of head binding may still seem repellent, it cannot be condemned as cruel. Twentieth century observers have frequently pointed out that European corsets, tapered shoes, and tight collars have caused more pain and permanent damage to their wearer than some of the more obviously bizarre body modifications practiced by non-European peoples.

The head alteration that archaeologists have discovered in the skeletal remains of the prehistoric Anasazi people of the southwestern United States may have been accidental. Infants were bound to flat wooden cradles, and most Anasazis thus grew to adulthood with flattened skulls. Since the Anasazi's living descendents no longer follow this practice, there is today no way of knowing whether the flattening process was consciously employed.

However, in the Pacific northwest two widely practiced types of head modification were unquestionably deliberate. The first involved flattening of both the forehead and the back of the skull, creating a wedge-shaped profile. The noted Canadian artist Paul Kane saw and painted several examples of persons with heads of this type. The woman shown here (cat. #13) was a member of the Cowichan tribe of lower Vancouver Island whom Kane painted in 1847. She holds her child, whose head is being shaped to resemble hers as a mark of high status. Slaves and commoners were not allowed to bind their heads.

An even more striking form of head shaping was practiced by the Kwakiutl of Vancouver Island, who wrapped infants' heads so as to lengthen them into a "sugar loaf" form. The forehead was also padded

13

14

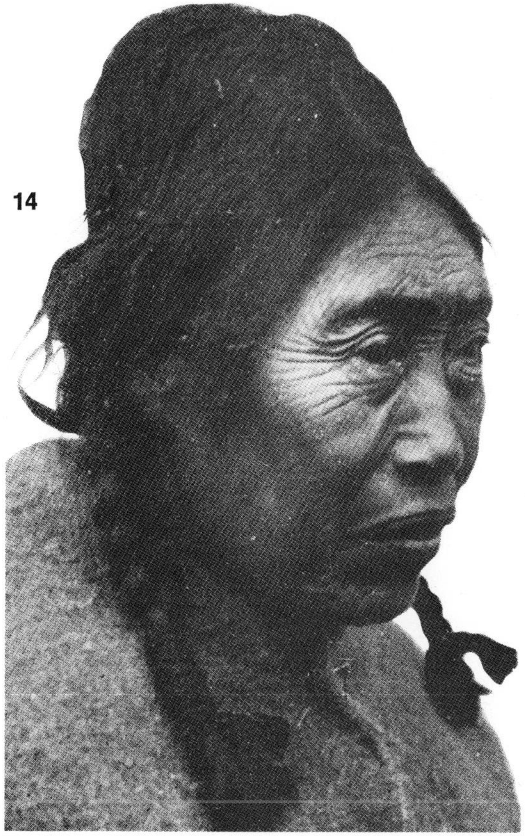

to augment the elongated effect. The woman shown here (cat. #14) with this kind of head alteration is thus marked as a member of an important family. The Kwakiutl themselves refer to this sort of person as one who has been "well cradled."

If head deformation was relatively uncommon in Native America, another type of body modification was widely followed. This was the practice of inserting ornaments into the body, usually the ears and nose. Besides opening the ear lobe, some peoples added one or more secondary piercings around the ear rim so that groups of dangling ornaments sometimes fringed the whole ear (cat. #15). This particular custom seems to have been most popular in the central United States and, like most other examples of ear and nose ornaments, appears to have functioned only as decoration.

Not content with piercing their ears and noses, Native Americans sometimes decorated their lower lips and chins with ornaments called "labrets." These were usually made of some substantial material like wood, ivory, stone, or bone. Eskimos, especially those in Alaska, often wear chin labrets like that of the young woman from Nunivak Island shown here (cat. #16). Hers are made of glass trade beads, but earlier chin labrets would have been ivory or bone. Eskimo women wear labrets solely for ornament, but women of the Northwest Coast wore lip labrets as marks of rank. A Haida mask (cat. #17) depicts an elderly woman with such an ornament, indicating that she belongs to a noble family.

These few examples will give some idea of the vast and complex range of body decoration practiced by native peoples throughout North America. The results, as we have seen, were often handsome and even a little startling at times. Their variety and beauty offer mute testimony to the wide purposes they served and the creative impulses from which they sprang.

Body Decoration

•1
Many Pipe Woman
Winold Reiss, American, 1888-1953.
Pastel and gouache on paper, 29½ x 21½ in.
This Blackfeet woman has painted both her hair part and forehead red. Daubs of yellow on her hair and painting on her chin complete this purely ornamental decoration.
The Anschutz Collection

2
Face Painting
Thompson River Salish, British Columbia.
The design belonged to a hunter named Tsala and was worn as a protection against grizzly bears.
After "Tattooing and Face and Body Painting of the Thompson River Indians" by J. A. Teit, *45th Annual Report of the Bureau of American Ethnology* (Washington, D.C., 1930), p. 43 and pl. 9e.

3
Face Painting
Haida, Queen Charlotte Islands, British Columbia.
From Dedans village. The design represents an eagle's nest. After "Facial Paintings of the Indians of Northern British Columbia" by Franz Boas, *Memoirs of the American Museum of Natural History* (New York, 1900), 1, 22 and pl. V, no. 10.

4
Face Stamp
Tlingit, Alaska, late 19th century.
Carved wood, 7¾ in.
The raven's foot design identifies those stamped with it as members of a raven lineage. Collected by George T. Emmons at Klukwan village.
Field Museum of Natural History,
Dept. of Anthropology 79077

5
Face Painting
Central and Southern Plains, contemporary.
Commercial cosmetics.
Each model has created the designs he customarily wears at social dances.
Courtesy Native American Education Project,
University of Colorado at Denver

•pictured in catalog

•6
Body Painting
Arapaho, Wyoming and Oklahoma.
The body painting and costume are worn by the Lodge Maker of the Sun Dance on the fourth day of the ceremony. The costume includes a native leather kilt and trade cloth overkilt, ornaments of sage, and an eagle wingbone whistle.
After *The Arapaho Sun Dance: The Ceremony of the Offerings Lodge* by George Dorsey, Field Museum of Natural History Anthropological Series (Chicago, 1903), IV, 161 and pl. CX.
Denver Art Museum Collection
Moccasins BAr - 31 Overkilt R - 41

7
Body Painting
Mandan, North Dakota.
The figure represents Okahida, the Owl Spirit or Evil One. This character, whose sinister name is misleading, appears during the fourth day of Okipa, the Medicine Lodge Ceremony.
After *O-Kee-Pa: A Religious Ceremony and Other Customs of the Mandans* by George Catlin (Yale University Press, 1967), pp. 59 f. and pl. IX.

8
Body Painting
Maricopa, Arizona
Eight dancers painted and costumed in this manner performed under the direction of two leaders for the Pan-neech festival which was observed at harvest time and on other occasions of importance or good fortune.
After "A Pima-Maricopa Ceremony" by Herbert Brown, *American Anthropologist,* n.s. 8 (Dec., 1906), 139-153.

•9
Facial Tattooing
Alaskan Eskimo.
This photograph of Daisy Okinello, a young woman of St. Lawrence Island, shows decorative tattoos on her cheeks, chin, hands, and forearms.
Denver Art Museum: Gift of Norman Potosky

•10
Body Tattooing
Unidentified tribe, Eastern Florida.
Engraving (1590) by Theodore de Bry, Flemish, after the field sketch (1564) by Jacques Le Moyne, French.
The subject is Saturiba, a 16th century chief.
The tattoos indicate his high rank.
From *The New World* by Stefan Lorant
(New York, 1946), p. 57.

16

•11
Body Tattooing
Haida, Queen Charlotte Islands, British Columbia.
The figure on the man's chest represents the bear and those on his forearms, the eagle. Properly read, these heraldic emblems tell us he is a person of high rank in the Eagle moiety and of a clan within this group that used a bear crest.
From "The Coast Indians of Southern Alaska and Northern British Columbia" by Ens. Albert Niblack, U.S.N., *Report of the U.S. National Museum for the Year ending June 30, 1888* (Washington, D.C., 1890), pl. V.

12
Body Tattooing
Hupa, Northern California.
The man is measuring native money (the marine shells *Dentalia pretiosa*) against tattooed marks on his forearm. The money's value increases according to its length.
From *Handbook of the Indians of California* by A. L. Kroeber, Bulletin 78 of the Bureau of American Ethnology (Washington, D.C., 1925), pl. XI.

•13
Caw-Wachem
Paul Kane, Canadian, 1810-1872.
Oil on canvas, 30 x 24⅞ in.
The subject is a Cowichan woman of lower Vancouver Island, British Columbia. Her deformed head was bound in infancy like that of the child in her arms. During his western journey in 1847-48, the artist observed many whose high status was indicated in this way.
Montreal Museum of Fine Arts 47.991
Photo courtesy of the Montreal Museum of Fine Arts

•14
Head Alteration
Kwakiutl, British Columbia.
The head of this elderly woman was bound in infancy to signal her high social status.
From "The Kwakiutl of Vancouver Island" by Franz Boas, *Memoirs of the American Museum of Natural History* (New York, 1908), VIII, 457 f. and pl. 36.

•15
Multiple Ear Ornaments
Winnebago, Wisconsin.
This woman wears several groups of silver ornaments set in multiple piercings around her ear rims.
Photo taken at Black River Falls, Wisconsin, about 1907.
Smithsonian Office of Anthropology Photo Collections, neg. 4403

•16
Chin Labrets and Nose Ring
Alaskan Eskimo.
The subject is Ugiyaku, a woman of St. Lawrence Island. Both sets of ornaments are glass trade beads. She wears a waterproof boat parka made of seal intestines.
From *The North American Indian* by Edward S. Curtis (Norwood, Mass., 1930), Supplemental Folio XX, pl. 693.

•17
Mask
Haida, Queen Charlotte Islands, British Columbia, c. 1880.
Carved wood with abalone shell ear ornaments and raveled fiber hair.
9 x 7¼ in.
The carving depicts an elderly woman with a labret in her lower lip.
Denver Art Museum NTI-4

18
Lip Labret
Alaskan Eskimo, late 19th century.
Fossil ivory, 1½ in.
Denver Art Museum: Gift of Norman Potosky 2667-10

19
Chin Labret
Alaskan Eskimo, St. Lawrence Island, early 19th century.
Ivory stained black, 1 in.
Denver Art Museum: Gift of Norman Potosky QEsk-374

20
Ear Ornaments
Prehistoric Mississippian Culture, Tennessee, c. 14th century.
Shell, 2¼ in. dia.
This large ornament shows the influences from Mexico often seen in prehistoric southeastern art.
Denver Art Museum JMB-1

21
Earrings
Coast Salish, Malahat Reserve, British Columbia, early 20th century.
Silver, 1¼ in.
A Victorian-inspired form.
Denver Art Museum JSl-1

22
Earrings
Kiowa, Oklahoma, late 19th century.
German silver, 2¾ in.
The design represents a stylized crawdad. Earrings of this sort were worn by men in pre-reservation times. Today they are often worn by participants in peyote meetings.
Denver Art Museum JKi-40

23
Earrings
Pawnee, Oklahoma, 1967.
German silver, 1⅛ in.
The form is called "ball and cone." This pair was made by Julius Caesar, a noted Pawnee silversmith, as a replica of a 19th century form.
Denver Art Museum: Gift of Norman Feder JPn-4

24
Earrings
Pawnee, Oklahoma, contemporary.
German silver, 1¼ in. dia.
Made by Julius Caeser (see #23).
Denver Art Museum: Gift of Richard Coulson JPn-6

25
Earrings
Potawatomi, Wisconsin, late 19th century.
German silver, 1⅛ in.
A traditional form from the Great Lakes area.
Denver Art Museum JPw-30

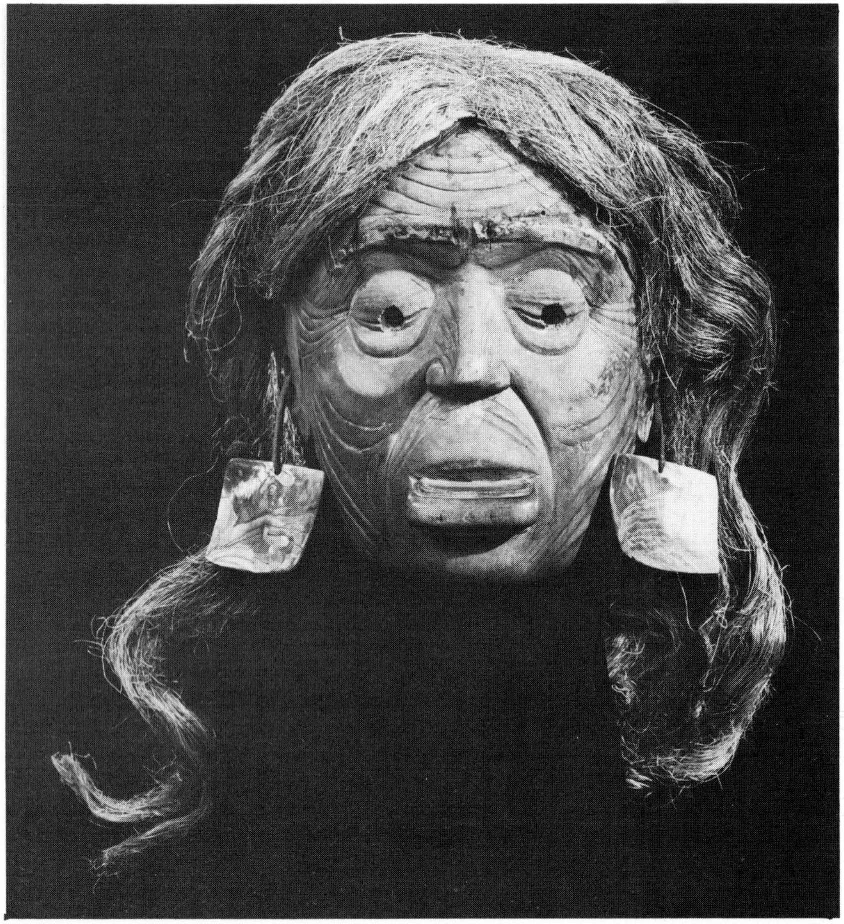

17

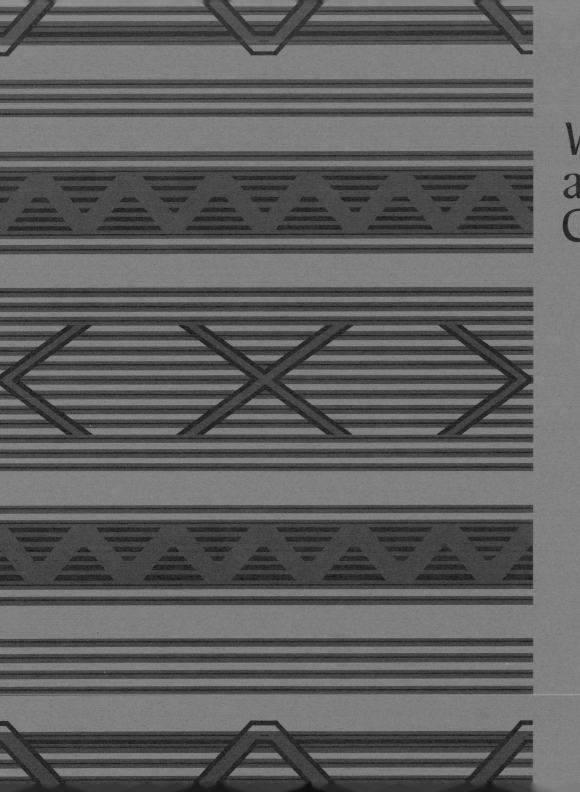

WRAPPED and Folded CLOTHING

Native American Clothing Traditions

For more than a century, writers have been publishing descriptions of the clothing and other personal decorations of various Native American peoples. So far, these reports have tended to particularistic approaches. Some have concentrated upon careful examinations of specific garments while others have analyzed the wardrobe of a particular group of people. Still others have emphasized the function of clothing in a certain society or have dissected the symbolism of decoration. One group of writers has offered directions for constructing replicas of native clothing. Although these studies have contributed much to our general knowledge, very few have attempted broad, synthetic examinations of Native American clothing aimed at illuminating its historical development or at determining the principles of its construction.

Those few works that have dealt wth North American native clothing on a broad scale have treated the subject as a springboard to some other problem. For example, Gudmund Hatt's well-known study of the native leather clothing of Eurasia and North America, first published in 1914, was aimed at discovering how man first settled the Eurasian land mass and subsequently the New World. Hatt saw in native leather clothing important historical evidence to support his conclusions, which have been fiercely defended and attacked ever since. His theories need not concern us here. It is enough to note that Hatt's primary interest was not in the leather clothing itself.

In this catalog and the exhibition it accompanies, articles of Native American clothing have been arranged according to the concepts of their basic construction. It has been possible to treat the subject in this way because a review of North American native dress shows that most garments are in fact variants of a few main ideas. Each of these ideas is referred to here as a "tradition." This term is to be understood in the sense of an archetypal custom that continues to influence the habits of later generations. It is not meant to imply that those garments falling within a given group must be directly related historically to one another. The only relationship is conceptual. By analogy, one could say that the pyramids of Mexico and Egypt are conceptually related since those who designed them chose to build in pyramid form. However, few responsible scholars would insist on a historical relationship between the two. Man has been an extremely mobile creature, meeting and exchanging ideas with his contemporaries in unexpectedly distant places. But he is also an inventive animal. Throughout history and in widely scattered geographical locations, he has created, forgotten, and rediscovered similar concepts. Knowing this, it is difficult to insist that all examples within any given "tradition" must have originated in the same source.

What are the "traditions" of Native American clothing design? The simplest is that of wrapped or draped clothing which the wearer often holds in place by hand although he might also tie or pin it into position. In complexity, fitted clothing stands at the opposite pole from simple wrapped garments, for garments in this tradition are cut of many pieces so as to follow the precise contours of the body: the natural hang of the arms, the differences in shape between back and chest. Because the aim of fitted clothing is just that — to achieve a good fit — each part of a garment is often unique. The back of a shirt is not cut like the front, the inside and outside sections of a sleeve are not alike, and so on. As a result, a fitted garment, whether an Eskimo parka or a business suit, will not lie flat. Indeed, it *cannot* since it was conceived as a three-dimensional construction.

Between the two extremes of wrapped and fitted clothing lies a tradition of garments sewn together of pieces meant only to approximate the form of the body. The native full-length leather dresses of the western United States are examples of this tradition. Each is composed of several pieces sewn into a flat, loose-fitting garment that bears some relation to the shape of a woman's body but does not fit her precisely. Garments of this group are characteristically constructed of two equal halves, with a front and back or inside and outside that are exactly alike in size and shape. Since they are conceived two-dimensionally, these garments will all lie flat and are easy to fold and store. Although several authors have previously classified and described wrapped and fitted clothing, those garments which are neither draped nor fitted have not been studied. In fact, they have received so little attention that no generic term has ever been devised for them. Drawing upon their tendency to be constructed in two identical parts, we shall refer to them here as the "binary" tradition.

57, 270 The designs in this Northwest Coast "nobleman's" robe and headdress represent his family crest.
Tlingit, Alaska.

Wrapped and Folded Clothing

The infant wearing a diaper, the man leaving his shower in a towel, the Roman in his toga, or Dorothy Lamour in a colorful sarong — all have one thing in common. They are wearing wrapped clothing, a garment made of one continuous piece of material that is wrapped around some part of the body and fastened. Some wrapped garments — blankets, for example — may be held in place by the hands. Others must be tied, pinned, or belted. In some instances, wrapped garments have been sewn into tubular shapes for convenience, but they differ from other wrapped garments only because they are fastened by this means before being donned.

One of the simplest and most widespread forms of wrapped clothing is the breechcloth, a strip of material drawn between a man's legs and held against his body at waist level by a cord or belt. Often, the ends of the breechcloth are brought over the belt to hang down in front and back like a pair of tiny aprons. In Native America, these breechcloth ends were often decorated. In the southwest, handwoven Pueblo cotton breechcloths were embroidered and sometimes tie-dyed. In the midwest and sometimes on the plains, trade cloth was frequently ornamented with beadwork (cat. #26) or ribbon appliqué (cat. #28).

Sandals, pieces of material tied to the feet, were worn most often in North America in the southwestern deserts and along the Pacific coast. The prehistoric southwestern people we call the Basketmakers wove beautiful sandals of cotton and other native fibers in modified basketry techniques. For excellence of workmanship and attractive decoration, no other Native American footwear has ever surpassed the sandals worn by these people.

Like the wrapped sandal, the wrapped moccasin is also made of one piece of material, but it is sewn into a tubular form and drawn over the foot instead of being tied under or around it. One type of wrapped moccasin worn on the north plains until the late 19th century is still worn in the Columbia River plateau today. It is made of one piece of leather, folded along the inside edge of the foot and sewn together along the outer. One half of the leather piece thus becomes the sole and the rest forms the upper. Since these moccasins are cut from soft, flexible leather, they soon take on the exact shape of the wearer's feet. Before sewing they are beaded over the instep area (cat. #83). Another type of wrapped moccasin appears to be unique to the Winnebago. In this case, the single leather piece is folded along the mid-line of the sole and sewn together around the toe and heel. The balance of the material forms a high cuff which folds forward over the toe, almost covering the foot (cat. #87). Today these cuffs are decorated with beadwork or ribbon appliqué. Earlier examples were probably decorated in quill or moosehair embroidery.

The turban-like headwear once worn by men in the midwest were simply long strips of homemade braided fabric wound about the head and topped off with a feather or some other ornament (cat. #68). The vegetable fibers and buffalo hair originally used for these braided bands were replaced in the mid-19th century by commercial yarn and white glass beads. Braided bands of almost the same size were also worn as waist sashes by both men and women, and small bands served as knee garters.

Throughout the eastern United States, the basic garment of native women was a wraparound skirt which was worn from Georgia north into Quebec and as far west as eastern Kansas. Prehistoric stone and ceramic sculptures from the east indicate that the wraparound skirt may, in fact, have been one of the most long-lasting and widely-worn of all Native American clothing forms. In what seems to be an unrelated invention, women of the central northwest coast had created a similar garment made of rectangular pieces of material folded around the waist and tied with a sash or belt.

Until the mid-18th century, these garments were made of native cloth or leather. Possibly a few women living adjacent to European traders had skirts of trade cloth. No examples of wraparounds made of native material exist today, but there are many drawings by European observers to show us how they looked. For instance, Simon DuPratz, a French artist who lived in Louisiana from 1718 until 1734, included in his sketchbook a drawing of two native women dressed only in wraparounds (cat. #30). In spite of such visual records, we can only guess how these skirts were decorated. Presumably the leather skirts were painted, possibly dyed black with walnut husks, and perhaps further embellished with porcupine quill or moosehair embroidery in the manner of surviving leather tobacco pouches and moccasins from the same period. Woven skirts may have been decorated with an ornamental weave or with some form of embroidery. Since the few surviving scraps of prehistoric southeastern cloth are painted, either directly or by a batik process, it is likely that the Hopewell and other early women of this region wore skirts of these materials. The wraparound skirts worn on the northwest coast were made of cedar bark, shredded into soft fibers and woven into various garments by a simple twining

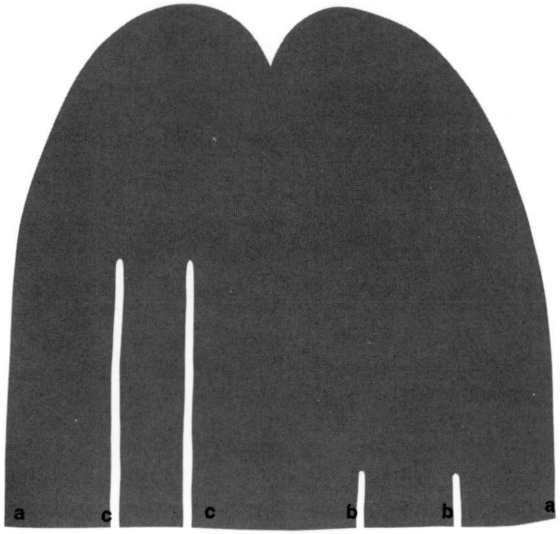

83

83

68

method. A number of these skirts still exist today but none is decorated. Since the mid-18th century, most wraparound skirts of the east have been made of European materials. The Iroquois women, for instance, favored fine dark blue broadcloth and embroidered it with beads (cat. #31). In the midwest, the Osage and their neighbors used a woolen material called "list cloth," which they decorated with beadwork and ribbon appliqué (cat. #32).

In prehistoric and early historic times, men of the southwestern Pueblos wore a short kilt resembling the eastern wraparound skirt as an everyday garment in warm weather. Since the mid-19th century, however, it has survived only as a ceremonial garment, hand-woven of native cotton and decorated with wool embroidery in figures referring to clouds, falling rain, and germinating crops (cat. #34). Since the assurance of life through a good harvest is an important concern of Pueblo religion, these kilts stand in an obvious relation to the ceremonial dances in which they are worn and, in fact, function as a kind of prayer in themselves.

Although the kilt is worn today only as a ceremonial garment, a related woman's garment has continued to serve both everyday and festival needs. This Pueblo woman's dress is a rectangle of cloth wrapped around the body, passing under the left arm and fastened over the right shoulder and down the right side (cat. #35). The fastening is achieved with coarse stitches of native yarn, silver brooches, or a combination of both. In prehistoric times, the dress was woven of native cotton dyed and decorated in various ways. Since the introduction of sheep, some examples have been hand-woven in wool. The borders of both cotton and wool dresses are ornamented by twill weaves or wool embroidery. At one time every pueblo had its distinctive dress border designs. Zuni, for example, favored black wool dresses with dark blue embroidery (cat. #37) while Acoma emphasized embroidery in several colors (cat. #38). Hopi wool dresses, on the other hand, often had blue borders worked in fine diamond twill (cat. #36). Unlike the sacred decorations on the ceremonial kilts, these dress embroideries are purely ornamental.

Until sometime in the 19th century, a garment similar to the Pueblo woman's dress was worn as an everyday costume by men of the Nootka and Kwakiutl. Made of the softened inner bark of the western red cedar (*Thuja plicata*) by a simple twining process, it was decorated, if at all, by a strip of fur woven into the upper border. The photographer Edward Curtis managed to locate a few of these garments for his models to wear when he visited Vancouver Island around 1914 (cat. #39), but today the few remaining examples are in museums.

An unusual kind of woman's dress, probably also derived from the wraparound skirt, was once worn along the upper Missouri River. By the 1830's, the form had become extinct, and only five examples survive today. So little is known of these garments that it is not even possible to say which groups wore them. The dress was made of one piece of leather (or several joined horizontally), folded

30

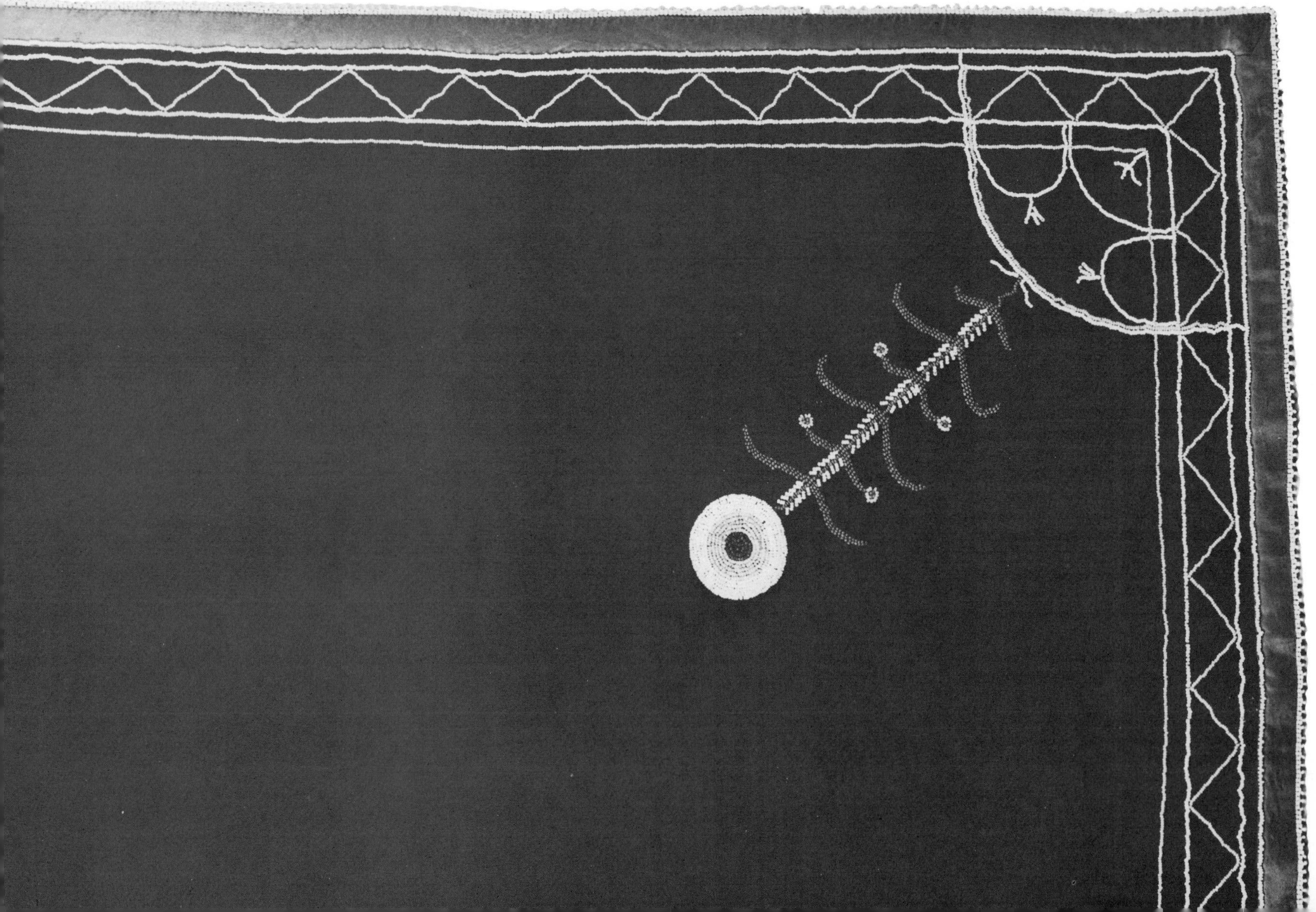

around the body and sewn closed down the side. The top portion of the dress was folded down to make a peplum and this in turn was cut vertically along the folded side for an arm opening. Shoulder straps or string ties held the dress in place (cat. #88).

Throughout much of Native America, both men and women wore some kind of leggings, *i.e.,* individual leg coverings supported by garters or tied to a belt. Generally, leggings were worn by men in combination with a breechcloth or kilt and by women with a long dress. Most leggings worn in North America belong to the tradition of wrapped clothing: a single piece of material is folded into a tubular form around the leg and tied or sewn closed. The knee-length leggings worn by women illustrate both of these methods of closing, as well as a technique of closure that combines sewing and tying (cat. #70 and 72).

Because the hip-length leggings worn by men sometimes required a whole deerskin apiece, the design of the garment was adapted to take advantage of the shape of the raw material. By the mid-19th century, a legging style based on this concept had become popular in central North America. The deerskin was folded from nose to tail and wrapped so that the fold ran down the inner leg. The head and neck regions of the hide were trimmed into a decorative cuff around the ankle, the front legs cut into fringe or pendants, and the hind legs used as tie strings to hold the legging to the wearer's belt. So trimmed, the deerskin was decorated and sewn or laced into a close-fitting garment. A popular Plains variation placed the seams at the sides and fringed the forelegs (cat. #75). In the midwest, men more frequently wore their whole deerskin leggings with the seams running straight up the front and the forelegs trimmed into decorative pendants (cat. #76). Obviously, most leggings constructed in this

35

36

37

38

39

pattern were made of leather, but the style persisted even after the introduction of trade cloth. Besides the "whole deerskin" leggings, Native America produced a good many cut more simply. Some of these were tapering tubes constructed from a piece of leather cut as an equilateral trapezoid (cat. #80). Others were made from approximate rectangles of leather (cat. #79) or cloth (cat. #81) cut wide enough to allow material for side flaps after the leg portion had been sewn or laced closed. On the plains, it was once popular to paint leather leggings with horizontal stripes that served as "battle stripes" (cat. #80) or with personal "medicine" symbols (cat. #75). Purely ornamental designs were also applied in quilling, beadwork, and ribbon appliqué.

All Native Americans had one wrapped garment in common — the robe or blanket which could serve as both body covering and ground cover. The earliest robes were undoubtedly tanned furs sewn together — a form still in use in the subarctic today. With the exception of bear skins, native groups used whatever animal hide was plentiful in their region. Among the Plains people, bison hides were frequently shaved and painted. These tribes developed standardized designs for robe paintings and rigid customs concerning their use. Geometric patterns, for instance, were painted by women, and stylized depictions of people and animals were painted by men. Furthermore, some designs were intended to be worn only by men and others only by women. The "feathered circle," for example, was a geometric design painted by a woman but worn by a man (cat. #41), perhaps because it seems to refer in a general way to the brave deeds performed in battle. Other painted robes explained, by means of stylized drawings of actual battle scenes, the specific exploits of a particular warrior. Outside the plains, large robes were generally painted in simple geometric designs.

79

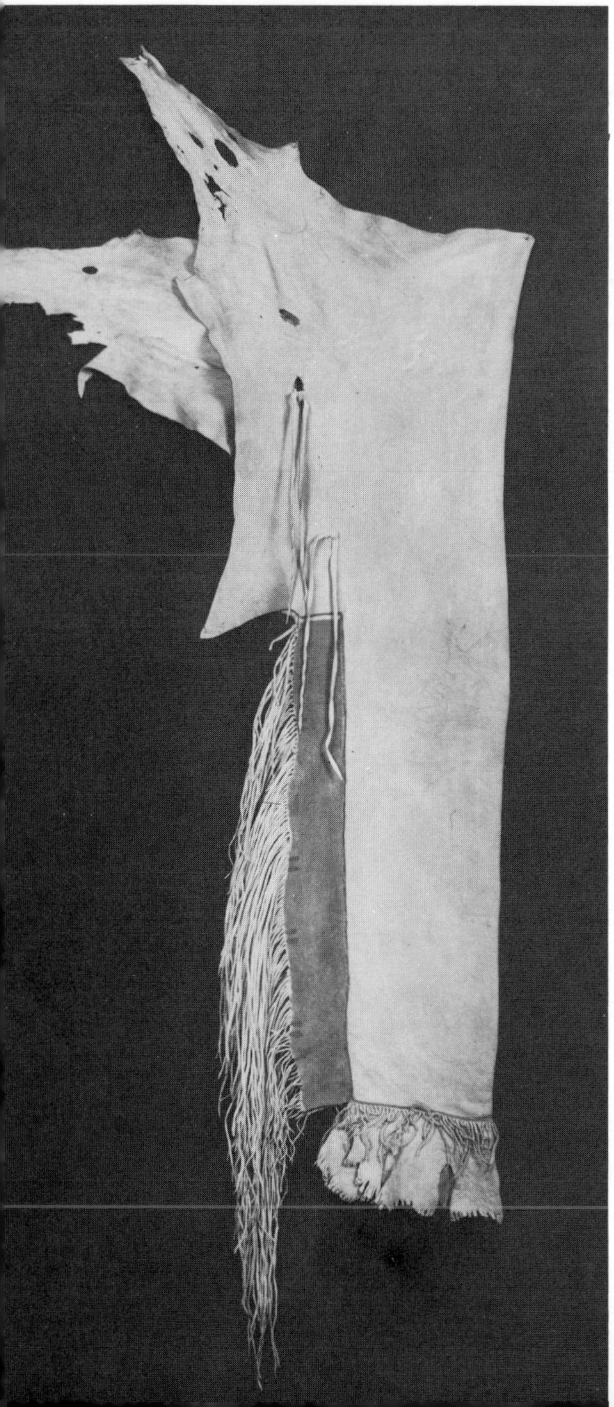

81

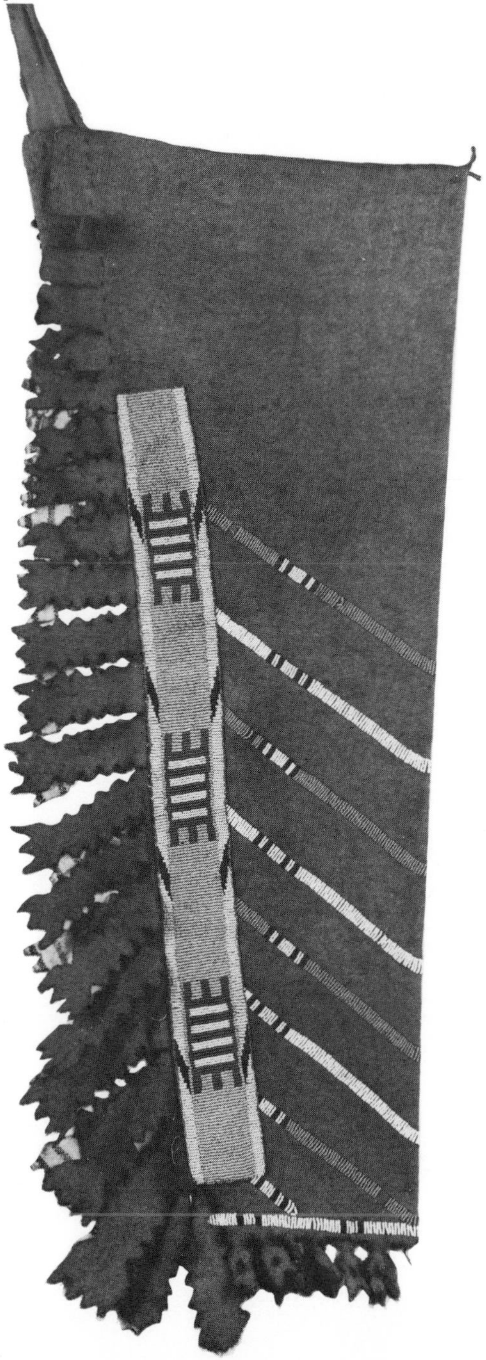

80

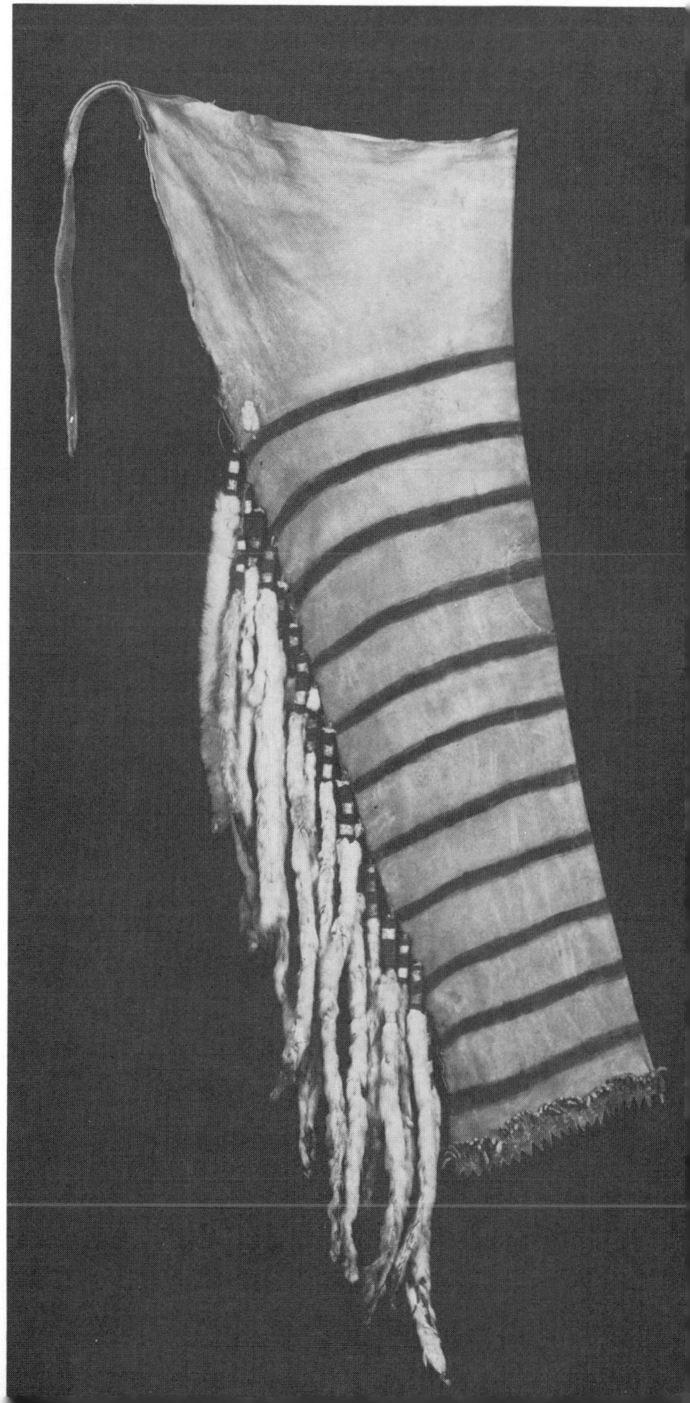

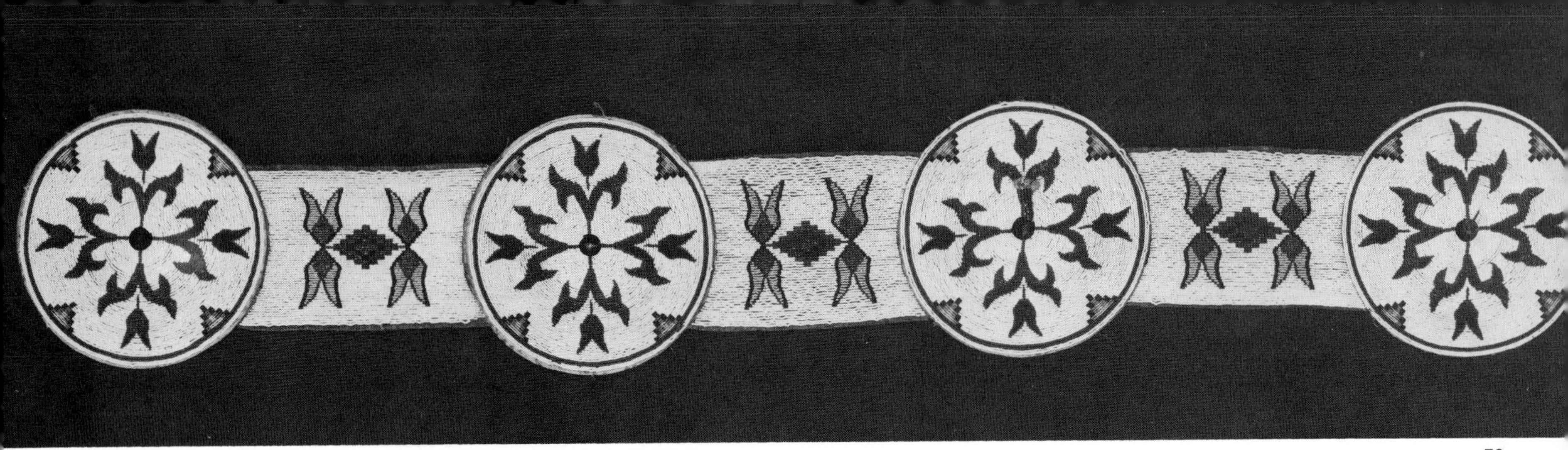

53

A popular robe ornament in both Plains and Plateau was the "blanket strip" (cat. #53). These bands of embroidery were sewn to the robe so as to appear in a horizontal position when in use. They were probably derived from the earlier custom of splitting a robe from head to tail for convenience in tanning. When the hide was prepared, the halves were sewn back together and some painting or embroidery added to conceal the seam.

Some Native Americans made fur robes. Among the northern Northwest Coast tribes and some adjacent inland peoples, many small animals' coats were sewn into a large winter blanket. Often, they were removed in one piece inside out (as a surgeon removes his rubber gloves), tanned, and then turned right side out again. Sewn together, they created a robe with fur on both sides. In the southwest and intermontane regions, furs — especially rabbit skins — were frequently cut into long strips and woven into blankets. The same thing was done in the north, particularly in central Canada, but with a process more like netting.

In the southeast, the iridescent feathers of wild turkeys were fashioned into shimmering robes. Powhatan and his famous daughter probably owned such garments. Turkey feathers were also made into soft, fluffy blankets in the prehistoric southwest by a special technique which involved stripping the vanes from the feather shafts and winding them around cordage which was to become the blanket warp. In California, feathers were inserted into fine netting to make thick blankets.

On the northwest coast, robes that might double as clothing or bedding were made from strands of softened bark twined together by the same method used for the bark wraparound skirts of this region. A few examples survive of large cedar bark robes with painted heraldic figures presumably worn in religious ceremonies, just as painted muslin dance blankets are worn today. The celebrated Chilcat blanket, named for the branch of the Tlingit which specialized in its manufacture, was twined by the same basic method used in cedar bark twining except that its fine weft threads were made of mountain goat wool. To achieve the curvilinear forms of the complex heraldic designs characteristic of this blanket, the worker had to use tapestry-like eccentric twining (cat. #57). Obviously, Chilcat blankets were not worn every day but only on ceremonial occasions and then only by Tlingit nobility.

The twining process by which Chilcat blankets and cedar bark garments were made is not a true form of weaving, but cloth woven of cotton and other natural fibers has been produced in North America since prehistoric times. The Pueblo people still weave cotton robes which are sometimes embroidered in wool (cat. #60). These people, who lived a settled life, were probably the first to experiment with wool from sheep introduced to the American southwest by Spanish colonists in the 17th century. In time, they passed both the material itself and instructions for weaving along to their Navajo neighbors, who, by the 19th century, were weaving fine examples of that best-known of all American textiles — the Navajo blanket (cat. #63 and 66). Navajo women continued to make light, flexible woolen

72

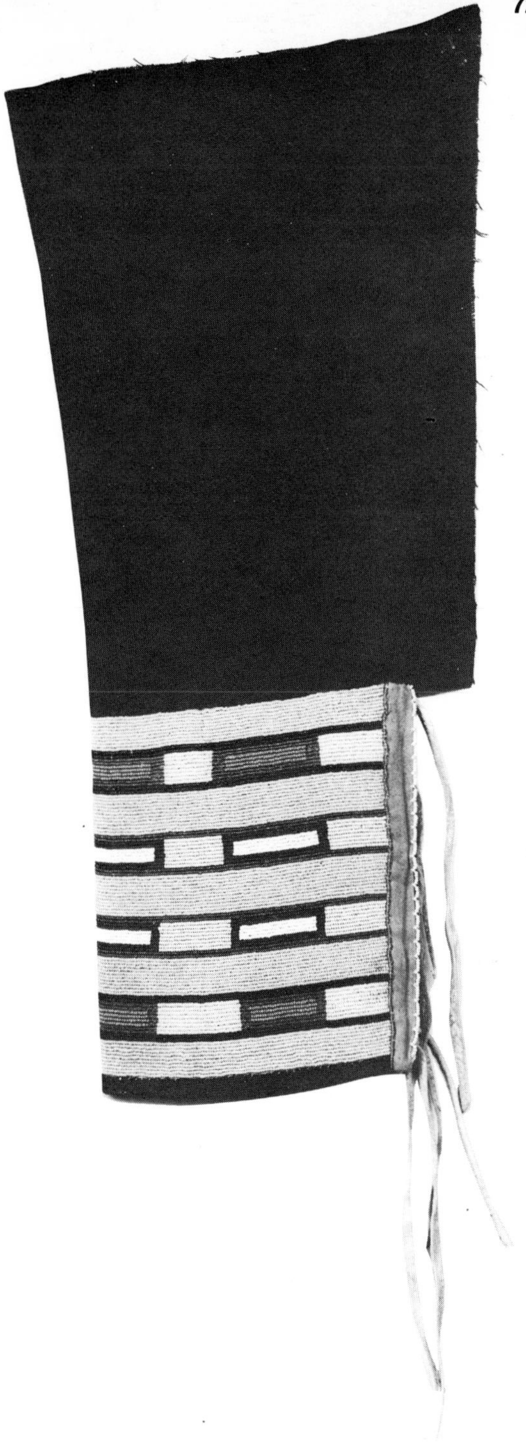

blankets and clothing until the late 19th century when, at the suggestion of American traders, they turned to coarser fabrics meant to be sold as rugs.

Trade cloth and blankets, made first in England and later in the United States, began to augment and then supplant native leather and cloth robes in the 18th century. To these foreign textiles the Native Americans applied their own distinctive ornaments or designs. The Plains tribes began to sew their beaded or quilled blanket strips to dark blue and red trade cloth. Those of the east and midwest adapted the designs that had been worked in quills or moosehair on leather to use in beadwork or ribbon appliqué on trade cloth. On the northwest coast, painted cedar bark robes were replaced by trade blankets decorated with flannel appliqué and rows of sparkling mother-of-pearl buttons. In each case, the decorative concepts of the earlier native robes were simply reinterpreted in European materials without altering their traditional functions. The purely decorative purpose of moosehair embroidery on leather midwestern robes could also be fulfilled in appliqué of silk ribbon on broadcloth (cat. #67). If designs painted on a cedar bark or leather robe of the Northwest Coast could refer to the owner's social status or personal spirit guardian, so might figures in flannel and buttons on a trade blanket (cat. #58).

88

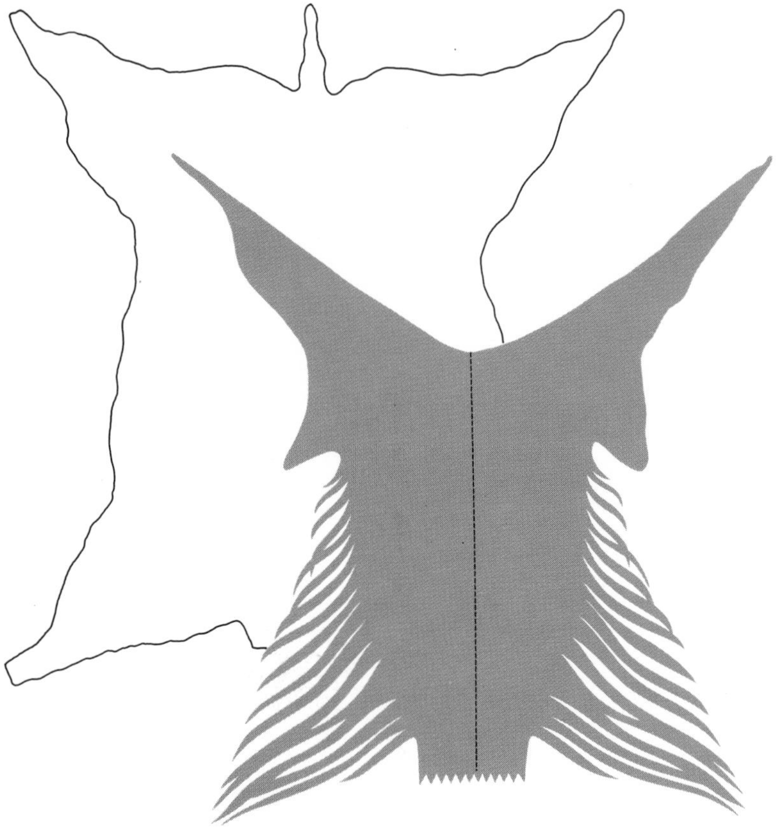

76, 89, 267 The beaded bands of his leggings, his grizzly claw necklace, and his shaved head help signal the warrior's honored position as a seasoned fighting man. Fox, Iowa.

Wrapped and Folded Garments

•26
Breechcloth
Oto, Oklahoma, 20th century.
Beadwork on list cloth, 63¼ x 20 in.
Most breechcloths are straight-sided, but this example is shaped for a more comfortable fit.
Denver Art Museum BO-2

27
Breechcloth
Zuni, New Mexico, late 19th century.
Native wool, plain twill center dyed indigo, diamond twill ends dyed black, 38½ x 10½ in.
A small example, probably made for a boy.
Denver Art Museum RZu-5

•28
Breechcloth
Winnebago, Wisconsin, late 19th century.
Silk ribbon appliqué on broadcloth, 50½ x 10 in.
The appliqué designs show the curvilinear forms that often occur in midwestern ribbonwork.
Denver Art Museum AWin-3

29
Sandals
Basketmaker, Tseahatso Cave, Canyon del Muerto, 6th century.
Apocynam and juniper fibers, 10¼ in.
An example of the fine woven sandals made in the prehistoric southwest.
Collected by Earl Morris.
University of Colorado Museum 10308

•30
Femme et Fille
Antoine Simon Lepage DuPratz, French, c. 1758.
Woodcut, size of original unknown.
The subjects are native women of Louisiana, where the artist lived from 1718-1734.
From *Southeastern Indians — Life Portraits* by Emma L. Fundaburk (Luverne, Alabama, 1958), fig. 103.

•31
Wraparound Skirt
Seneca, New York, 1936.
Beadwork and ribbon trim on broadcloth, 58 x 48 in.
Made at Tonawanda Reservation under the auspices of a FERA project.
The preference for light-colored beading on a dark garment is a survival of the earlier fashion for quillwork on leather dyed brownish-black with native dyes. The "tree of life" design was a favorite for the outer corner of skirts.
Denver Art Museum BSen-3

•32
Wraparound Skirt
Osage, Oklahoma, 20th century.
Beadwork and silk ribbon appliqué on list cloth, 56 x 77 in.
The placement of decoration shows that the skirt was meant to be worn folded, thus creating the impression of an overskirt.
Denver Art Museum BOs-25

•33
Woman's Costume with Wraparound Skirt
Menomini, Wisconsin, mid-19th century.
Silk ribbon appliqué on broadcloth, 55 x 60 in.
The skirt shows both the curvilinear and rectilinear types of ribbonwork design. The entire costume is typical of those worn by Menomini women in the mid-19th century.
Denver Art Museum AMen-1

•34
Kilt
Nambe Pueblo, New Mexico, 20th century.
Wool embroidery on native cotton cloth, 42 x 20½ in.
Worn by men in ceremonial dances. The embroidered designs represent terraced rain clouds and falling rain.
Denver Art Museum RNb-1

•35
Wraparound Dress
Hopi, Arizona, late 19th century.
Native wool cloth: center is plain twill in natural black and borders are diamond twill dyed indigo, 49 x 40 in.
Denver Art Museum RHc-73

•36
Wraparound Dress
Hopi, Arizona, late 1930's.
Native wool cloth: center is plain twill in natural black and borders are diamond twill dyed indigo, 53 x 38½ in.
Denver Art Museum RHc-83

•37
Wraparound Dress
Zuni Pueblo, New Mexico, late 19th century.
Embroidery in indigo-dyed wool yarn over natural dark native wool cloth in plain twill, 53 x 41 in.
The monochrome embroidery with stylized floral forms was once unique to Zuni Pueblo. The art is extinct today.
Denver Art Museum RZu-1

•pictured in catalog

•38
Wraparound Dress or Shawl
Acoma Pueblo, New Mexico, late 19th century.
Wool yarn embroidery over natural dark native wool cloth in plain twill, 56 x 40 in.
The heavy polychrome embroidery, once typical of Acoma Pueblo, is no longer made. This garment might be worn as a dress or outer shawl.
Denver Art Museum: Gift of Alfred I. Barton RAc-21

•39
The Whaler — Clayoquot
Edward S. Curtis, American, 1868-1952.
Sepia photograph, 22 x 18 in.
The Nootka man wears a wrapped garment of shredded cedar bark, formerly an everyday garment among his people.
From *The North American Indian* by Edward S. Curtis (Norwood, Mass. 1916), Supplemental Folio XI, pl. 394.

40
Cedar Bark Wraparound Garment
Nootka, Vancouver Island, British Columbia, late 19th century.
Twined native fabric of shredded cedar bark and mountain goat wool, 69 x 46 in.
See #39.
Denver Art Museum: Gift of Denver Museum of Natural History YNu-21

•41
Buffalo Robe
Sioux, Dakotas, c. 1870.
Native painting on tanned buffalo hide, 92 x 74 in.
The design, painted by women, is called the "feathered circle" or "black bonnet."
Denver Art Museum PS-39

42
Buffalo Robe
Sioux, Dakotas, c. 1870.
Native and trade paint on tanned buffalo hide, 78 x 68 in.
The design, called the "box and border," was painted and worn only by women.
Denver Art Museum PS-23

43
Mountain Sheep Robe
Blackfeet, Montana and Alberta, late 19th century.
Trade paints on tanned mountain sheep hide, 58 x 55 in.
The figures represent the war experiences of Big Sorrel Horse.
Denver Art Museum PBI-29

44
Cowhide Robe
Crow, Montana, early 20th century.
Beadwork on tanned cowhide, 100 x 74 in.
The Crow call this garment a "wedding robe." It is a post-reservation version of an earlier quilled buffalo robe sometimes made for a bride as part of her dowry.
Denver Art Museum BCr-92

45
Deerskin Robe
Crow, Montana, early 20th century.
Beadwork on tanned deerskin, 51 x 49 in.
A small version of #44, made for a little girl.
Denver Art Museum BCr-80

46
Elk Robe
Crow, Montana, c. 1930.
Quilled blanket strip on tanned elkhide, 73 x 72 in.
The leather robe with a strip of decoration was common on the plains in the 19th century and is still made occasionally. The strip of quillwork runs horizontally when the garment is worn.
Denver Art Museum VCr-6

47
Deerskin Robe
Sioux, Dakotas, c. 1890.
Beaded blanket strip on tanned deerskin, 70 x 64 in.
Made for a man and worn with the beaded strip running horizontally.
Denver Art Museum BS-149

48
Courting Blanket
Sioux, Dakotas, late 19th century.
Beaded blanket strip on strouding, 108 x 72 in.
Half-red and half-blue robes were reportedly worn by Sioux men engaged in formal courtship. Strouding is an English wool cloth, widely traded in North America.
Denver Art Museum BS-136

41

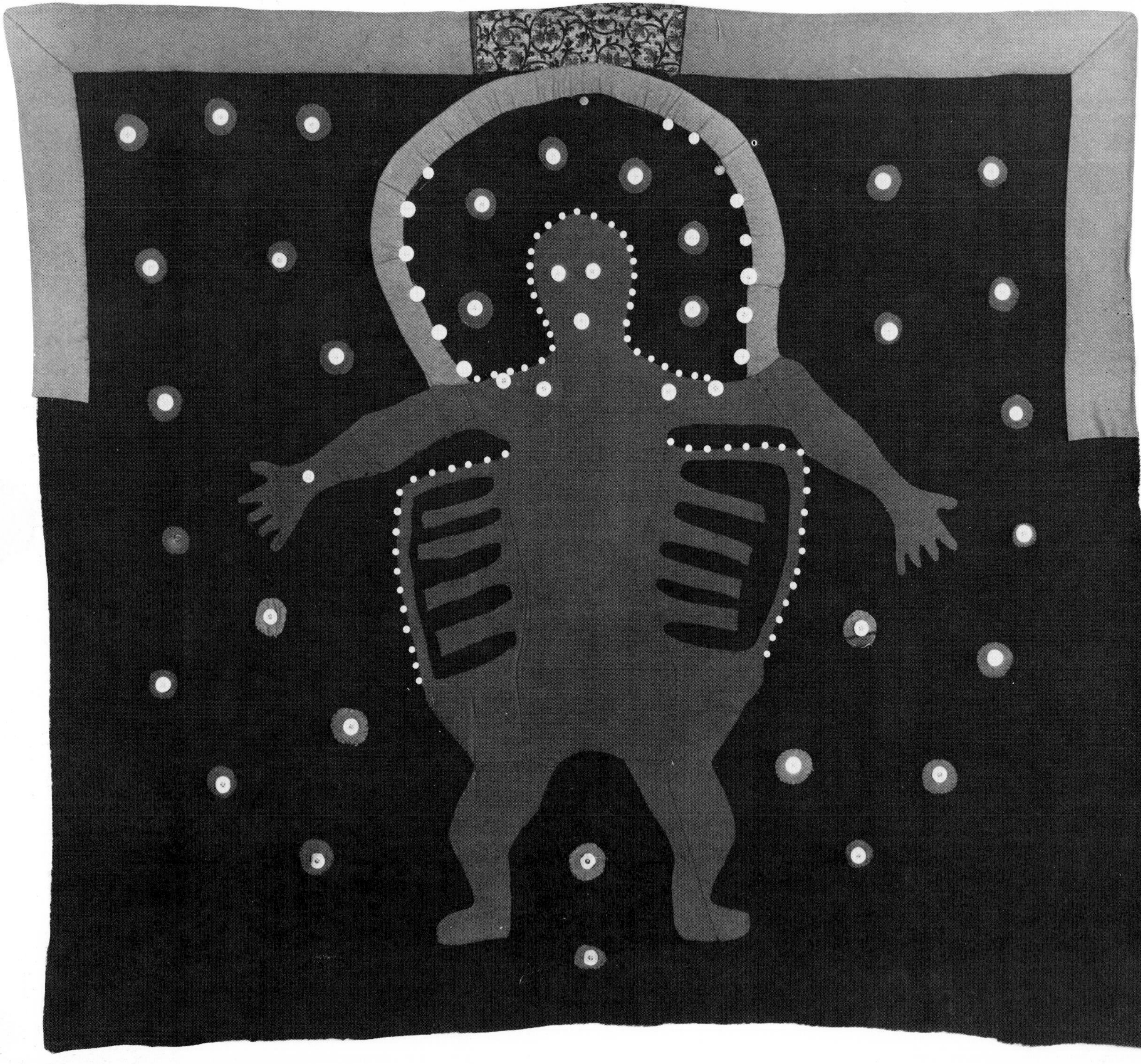

49
Blanket
Sioux, Dakotas, early 20th century.
Beaded blanket strip on strouding, 103½ x 66 in.
A man's blanket that belonged to Useful Heart, an Oglala of Pine Ridge Reservation.
Denver Art Museum BS-116

50
Blanket Strip
Sioux, Dakotas, c. 1870.
Beadwork on leather, 60 in.
Large buffalo hides were formerly slit lengthwise for convenience of handling during the tanning process. Afterward the halves were sewn back together and the seam covered with a band of quillwork. Blanket strips are thought to have developed from this practice.
Denver Art Museum BS-75

51
Blanket Strip
Crow, Montana, c. 1870.
Beadwork on buffalo leather, 48½ in.
The beadwork with its wide palette of colors and long, triangular forms is typically Crow of the late 19th century. See #50.
Denver Art Museum BCr-104

52
Blanket Strip
Shoshone, Idaho and Wyoming, late 19th century.
Beadwork on leather, 61 in.
The Shoshone lived on the margins of the Plains, and this example of their art shows both Crow and Cheyenne influence. See #50.
Denver Art Museum BSs-15

•53
Blanket Strip
Assiniboine, Alberta, c. 1920.
Beadwork on leather, 60 in.
The Assiniboine call these extra-wide blanket strips "stoles." Today they are carried by men and women as accessories to festival costumes. The stoles are no longer sewn to blankets but have become an entity unto themselves. See #50.
Denver Art Museum: Gift of F. H. Douglas BAs-8

54
Blanket Strip
Ute, Colorado and Utah, late 19th century.
Beadwork on leather, 69 in.
See #50.
Denver Art Museum BU-30

55
Fur Robe
Paiute, Nevada, 1938.
Twisted strips of rabbit skin in plain weave, 61 x 45 in.
Made especially for the Federal Indian Exhibit at the San Francisco World's Fair in approximation of a type formerly very common.
Denver Art Museum FPu-1

56
Feather Robe
Maidu, California, c. 1830.
Duck feathers on base of braided leather strands, 58 x 44 in. Collected by Captain John Sutter in the late 1830's. Using the feathers of over 200 birds, six women worked four months to make such a robe. Few examples of this rare form survive today.
Denver Art Museum FMa-1

•57
Chilcat Blanket
Tlingit, Alaska, late 19th century.
Mountain goat wool and shredded cedar bark in twined weave, 70 x 34 in.
Collected at Douglas Island, Alaska, in 1890. The central field depicts a diving whale while the lateral fields represent ravens. Animal forms are abstracted to some degree in order to accommodate them to the format of the blanket.
Denver Art Museum: Gift of Mr. and Mrs. Leonard Eicholtz RC-1

•58
Button Blanket
Tsimshian, British Columbia, c. 1910.
Red flannel and mother-of-pearl button appliqué on wool trade blanket, 52½ x 59 in.
The figures of Tsimshian blankets often depict the owners' guardian spirits. Ordinarily button blankets show family crests.
Denver Art Museum ATs-1

67

59
Button Blanket
Kwakiutl, Vancouver Island, British Columbia, 20th century.
Flannel and button appliqué on wool trade blanket, 72 x 53 in.
The crest design represents a whale. The blanket belonged to Willie Seaweed, a noted carver of Alert Bay, B.C.
Denver Art Museum AKw-2

•60
Cotton Robe
Acoma Pueblo, New Mexico, late 19th century.
Wool embroidery on native cotton cloth, 57 x 45½ in.
The pine tree figures are an unusual motif in Pueblo embroidery. Such robes are usually worn by women.
Denver Art Museum RAc-9

61
Blanket
Hopi, Arizona, 1950.
Native wool cloth in natural colors, 57 x 36½ in.
Although this is a recent example, Hopi plaid blankets are an old form. The small size indicates it was made as a boy's blanket.
Denver Art Museum: Gift of F. H. Douglas RHb-16

62
Blanket
Hopi, Arizona, late 1870's.
Native wool cloth in natural colors plus indigo, 46½ x 64 in.
The plain stripe design is an old Southwestern form, often called the "Moki stripe" because of its association with the Hopi.
Denver Art Museum: Gift of C. W. Douglas RHb-8

•63
Blanket
Navajo, Arizona, mid-19th century.
Native wool and Saxony in natural and dyed colors, 62 x 45 in.
The design is the second phase of the well-known "Chief" pattern. This textile was taken in trade for food by a pioneer Denver grocer in the 1860's.
Denver Art Museum: Gift of George Steele RNch-55

64
Blanket
Navajo, Arizona, c. 1860.
Native wool cloth in natural colors with indigo, 46½ x 83 in.
A textile from the Navajo Classic period. The extensive use of blue is unusual.
Denver Art Museum: Gift of Alfred I. Barton RN-146

60

65
Blanket
Navajo, Arizona, mid-19th century.
Handspun and Bayeta yarns; natural white, indigo and cochineal dyes, 60 x 84 in.
An outstanding example of Navajo Classic design.
Denver Art Museum RN-92

•66
Blanket
Navajo, Arizona, c. 1860.
Handspun yarns with natural and commercial dyes, 50 x 74½ in.
Another excellent example of Navajo Classic design.
Denver Art Museum; Gift of Alfred I. Barton RN-145

•67
Blanket
Miami, Indiana and Oklahoma, mid-19th century.
Ribbon appliqué on broadcloth, 59 x 51 in.
The alternating blocks of color are often seen in Miami ribbonwork. Blankets of this kind are generally worn by women.
Milwaukee Public Museum 31940/7765
Photo courtesy of the Milwaukee Public Museum

•68
Not-chi-mi-ne, an Ioway Chief
Unknown lithographer after portrait by Charles B. King, 1837.
Hand-colored lithograph on paper, 14 x 20 in.
The subject wears a wrapped native-made yarn turban surmounted by a headdress of deer and porcupine hair.
Denver Art Museum: Bequest of F. H. Douglas IP-61

69
Woman's Leggings
Blackfeet, Alberta and Montana, late 19th century.
Beadwork on canvas, trade cloth tops, 14½ x 13 in.
In use, these leggings covered the leg from ankle to knee and were tied along the outside. Blackfeet beadwork design emphasizes rectangular figures.
Denver Art Museum: Gift of Mrs. Harry Stoever BBI-88

•70
Woman's Leggings
Blackfeet, Alberta and Montana, late 19th century.
Beadwork on leather with cloth binding, 15 in.
Another example of Blackfeet design emphasizing squares and right-angled forms. Made by Mrs. Day Rider.
Denver Art Museum BBI-32

•71
Woman's Leggings
Cheyenne, Montana and Oklahoma, 1890's.
Beadwork on leather, 17 in.
The stepped blue triangles are a distinctive Cheyenne design. These leggings were made for a small girl.
Denver Art Museum BChy-20

•72
Woman's Leggings
Crow, Montana, late 19th century.
Beadwork on canvas, cloth tops, 20½ in.
The horizontal stripes may be derived from the earlier practice of painting women's garments with stripes to signify their husbands' war honors.
Denver Art Museum BCr-63

73
Woman's Leggings
Ojibwa, Western Great Lakes, mid-19th century.
Beadwork on broadcloth, 13 in.
The openwork designs are probably based on earlier quill or moosehair embroidery patterns.
Denver Art Museum BOj-21

74
Woman's Leggings
Ottawa, Michigan and Ontario, mid-19th century.
Ribbon appliqué on broadcloth, 18½ in.
The fine designs are typical of 19th century Great Lakes ribbonwork.
Denver Art Museum AOt-2

•75
Man's Leggings
Pawnee, Nebraska and Oklahoma, c. 1860.
Painted leather with horsehair trim, 32 in.
Celestial phenomena, especially the morning star, are important in Pawnee mythology. The painting may have been inspired by a vision.
Denver Art Museum LPn-3

•76
Man's Leggings
Midwestern United States, c. 1860.
Beadwork on leather, 38 in.
An unusual construction with bottom flaps covering the feet. The beaded forms are representative of midwestern abstract floral designs.
Denver Art Museum BSF-27

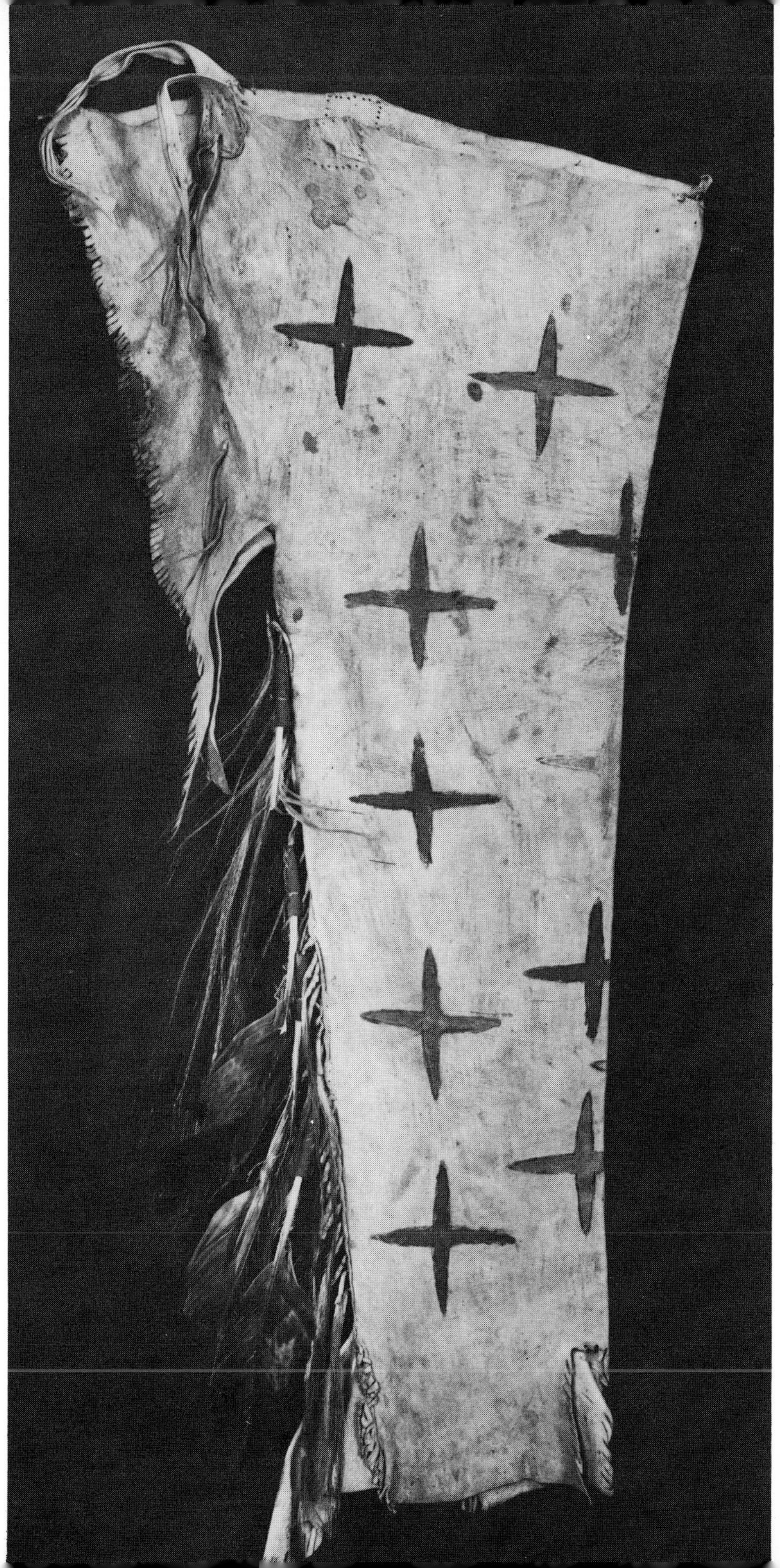

75

26

77
Man's Leggings
Ojibwa, Western Great Lakes, c. 1850.
Beadwork and ribbon on trade cloth, 27 in.
A cloth form based on the earlier leather pattern accommodating a whole deerskin.
Denver Art Museum ROj-27

78
Man's Leggings
Central Plains, c. 1840.
Painted leather with various ornaments, 44 in.
The painted stripes and locks of human hair refer to the military exploits of the wearer. The hair, which probably did not come from his victims, indicates that he has killed an enemy in battle, and the stripes signify war honors. The leggings are cut in the "whole deerskin" pattern.
Denver Art Museum LS-12

•79
Man's Leggings
Jicarilla Apache, New Mexico, late 19th century.
Painted leather, 39 in.
An example of man's leggings cut with narrow side flaps.
Denver Art Museum: Gift of the Estate of F. H. Douglas LAJ-12

•80
Man's Leggings
Blackfeet, Alberta and Montana, late 19th century.
Painted leather with ermine tubes, 30 in.
Another example of painted stripes indicating war honors. The northern Plains people often decorated clothing with strips of ermine fur sewn into tubular pendants.
Denver Art Museum PBI-11

•81
Man's Leggings
Sarsi, Alberta, late 19th century.
Beadwork on strouding, 30½ in.
Unaccustomed to working with cloth, Native Americans found it easier to cut along thread lines and thus tended to work in rectangular pieces. The wide side flaps shown in this example resulted from this rectangular approach to cloth-handling.
Denver Art Museum BSar-1

82
Boy's Leggings
Eastern Plains, c. 1830.
Silk ribbon appliqué on list cloth, 22 in.
The cut is related to the earlier "whole deerskin" form (see #78). These leggings were collected in 1832-33 by a European nobleman visiting North America.
Denver Art Museum AS-4

•83
Western Folded Moccasin
Northern Plains or Plateau, mid-19th century.
Pony beads on buffalo leather, 10 in.
An early example of a moccasin made by folding the leather along the side of the foot.
Denver Art Museum B-155

84
Western Folded Moccasins
Spokane, Washington, late 19th century.
Beadwork on leather, 5½ in.
Another example of the pattern described above (#83).
The "scatter" beading is unique to the Plateau.
Denver Art Museum BSp-1

85
Western Folded Moccasins
Coeur d'Alene, Idaho, late 19th century.
Beadwork on leather, 9¾ in.
A fully beaded example of this pattern, decorated in imitation of northern Plains moccasins.
Denver Art Museum: Gift of John D. Green BCdA-8

86
Midwestern Folded Moccasins
Winnebago, Wisconsin and Nebraska, late 19th century.
Ribbon appliqué and beadwork on leather, 10½ in.
An outstanding feature of this unusual pattern is the high, folded front cuff.
Denver Art Museum AWin-8

•87
Midwestern Folded Moccasins
Winnebago, Wisconsin and Nebraska, early 20th century.
Beadwork on leather, 7½ in.
Note the similarity of the beadwork designs to those of the ribbonwork on the preceding example.
Denver Art Museum BWin-22

•88
Old North Plains Dress
Replica by the Denver Art Museum Workshop.
Beadwork on painted leather, 46 in.
The original from which this replica was copied is in the Peabody Museum at Harvard University. It was collected in 1804 by Lewis & Clark on the Upper Missouri River. The pattern is unusual and little is known of its development.
Denver Art Museum BPiC-4

71

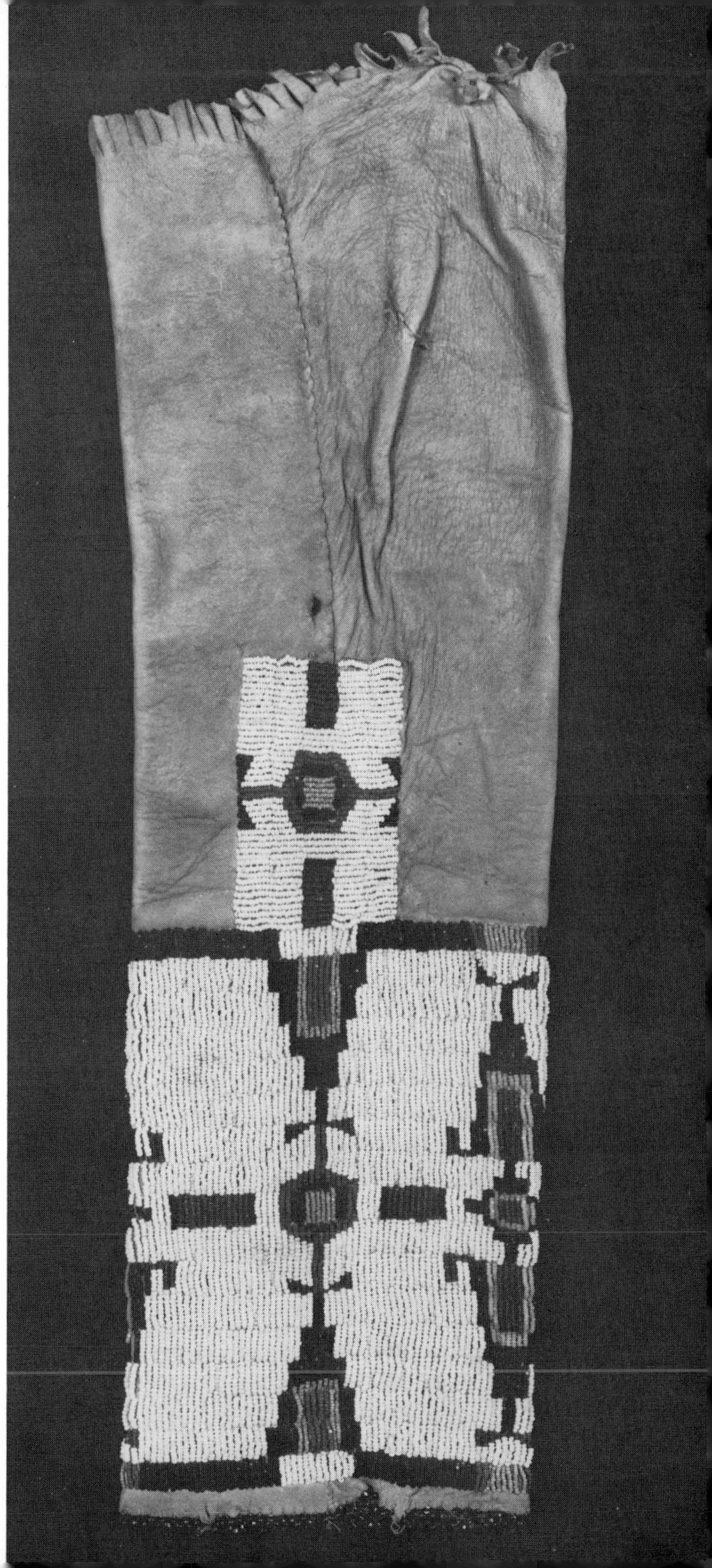

70

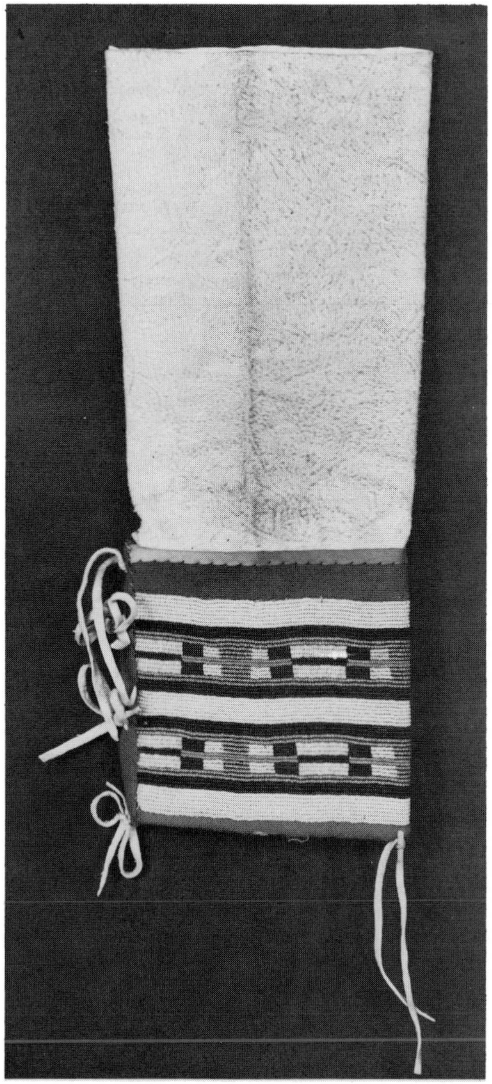

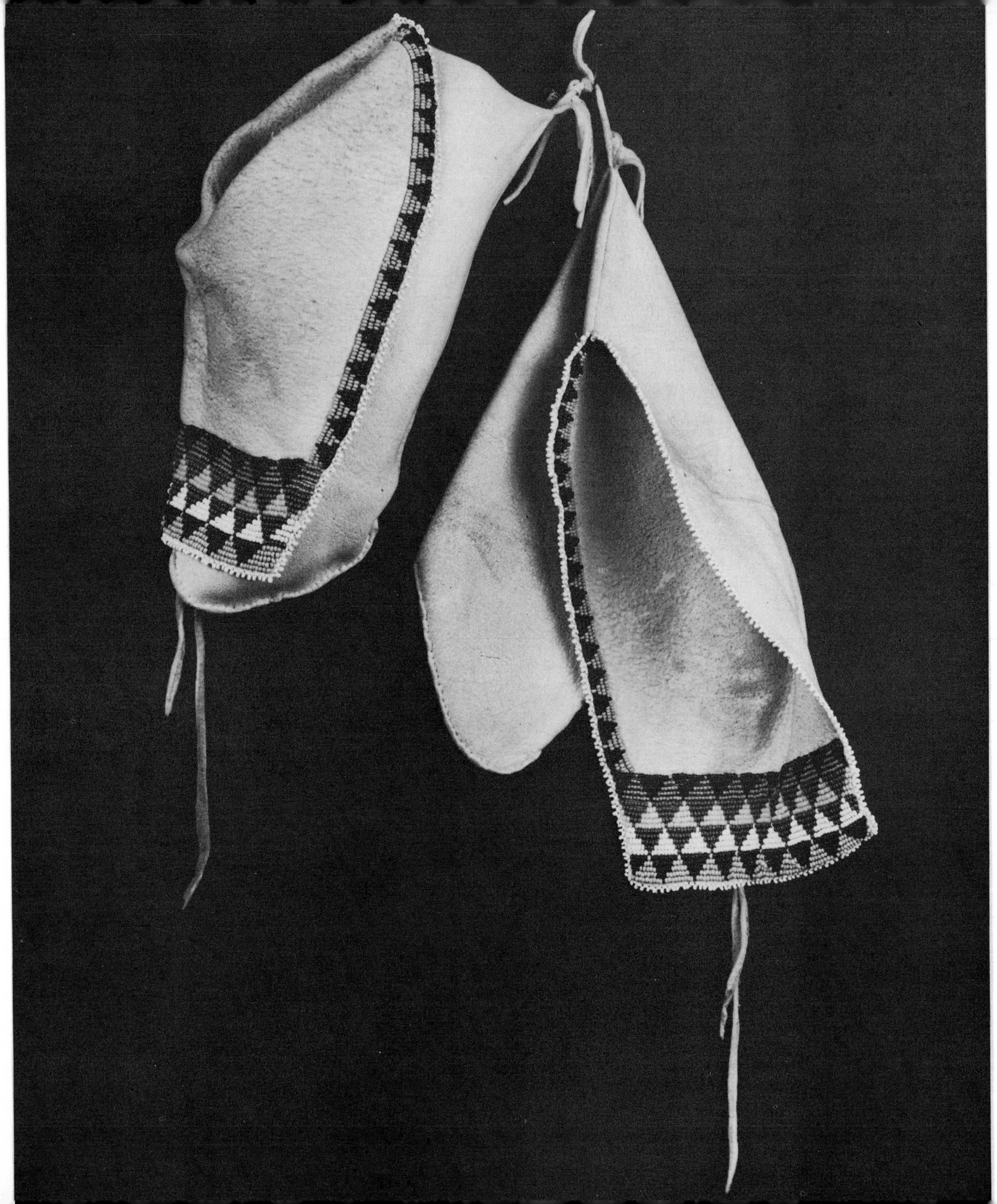

87

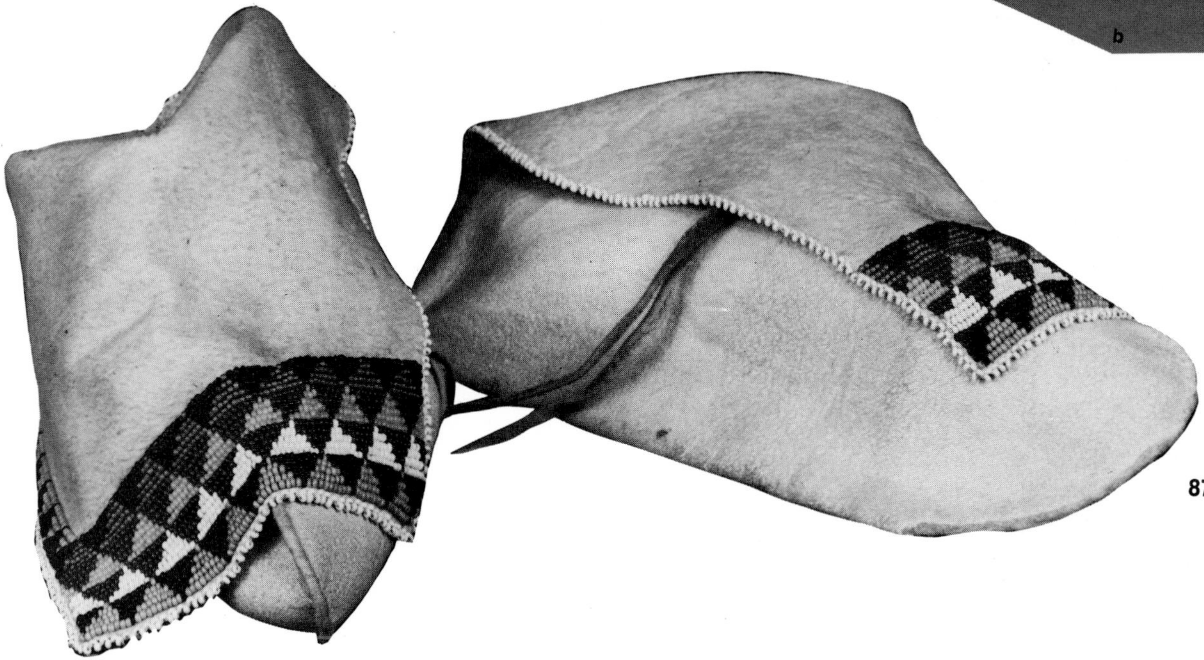

87

BINARY CLOTHING

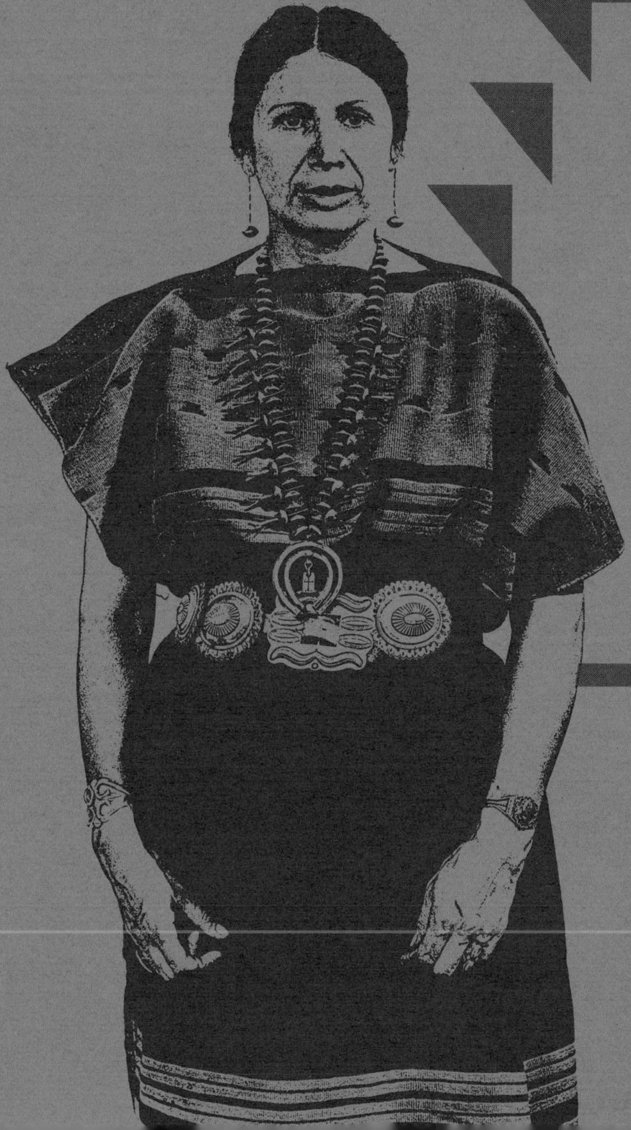

Binary Clothing

Anything made or existing in two sections is said to be "binary," a term particularly well-suited to describe those native garments that are neither folded about the body nor fitted to it. We have adopted the term here to define a category of clothing so little noticed that no generic word has ever been coined to describe its construction. In the case of Native American garments, those that belong to the binary tradition are torso coverings of some sort. Their two main parts are inevitably the front and the back, which are usually the same approximate size and shape. When the two halves of a binary garment are joined at the shoulders, they are almost always sewn or tied along a straight line. When other parts, such as sleeves, are added, they too are joined in a straight seam. As a result, binary garments do not fit closely but tend instead to be loose and a bit full.

The simplest, and undoubtedly the oldest, examples of binary clothing from Native America are not sewn at all. These are double aprons, rectangular pieces of cloth or leather worn around the waist and tied together by their top corners at the wearer's sides. One apron thus covered the front of the body to about mid-thigh, and the other covered the corresponding part of the back. Women, who wore such aprons as undergarments, didn't bother to decorate them; but the aprons worn by men as an alternate to the breechcloth were often decorated (cat. #89) and worn with matching leggings.

89

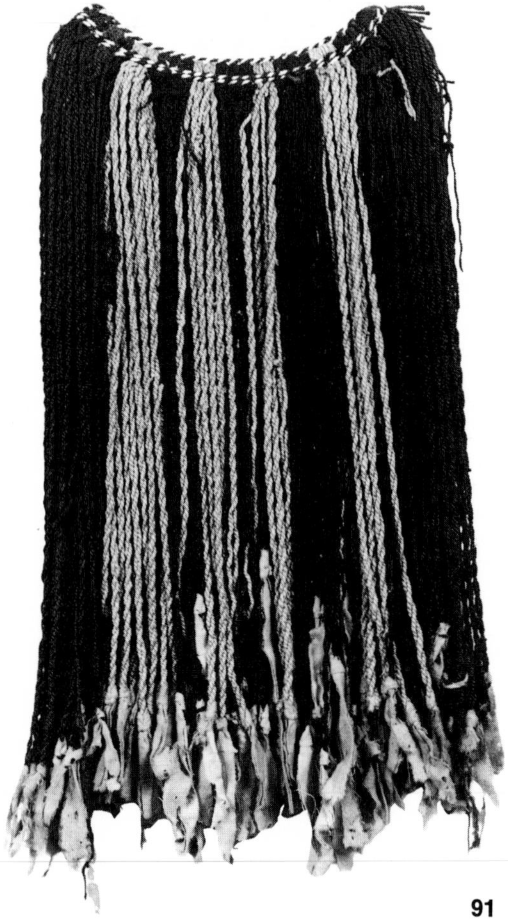

91

Very similar to the double apron were the double fringe skirts worn by the native women of both coasts. These garments resemble the Polynesian grass skirt except they were made in two parts and tied together at the woman's sides. Native vegetable or animal fibers were laid out vertically like warp strands on a loom and joined horizontally in courses of simple twining to a depth of five or six inches. The untwined portion of the fibers hung as a loose fringe to the woman's knees. On the eastern seaboard, fringe skirts were frequently made of Spanish moss or softened basswood fibers. On the west coast, tule, sagebrush bark, and similar materials were used, and wealthy native women in the Pacific northwest wore fringe skirts of native wool. Mojave women along the lower Colorado River made particularly elaborate fringe skirts (cat. #91). The front section was made of strands of red and dark blue trade cloth ravelled into long strings and then twisted into simple cord. To this the Mojave added a final fillip: the back section, made of softened and finely shredded willow bark, was twined very fully to create a "bustle" effect.

From northwestern California, where the accumulation of wealth was regarded as a sacred activity and the possession of property as proof of industry and virtue, come the most elaborate double skirts made in Native America. Unlike most binary garments, these handsome ceremonial skirts were made by the Yurok and neighboring groups from two pieces of material of unequal size. The back skirt is an entire deerskin folded laterally to cover the woman's back and sides with a double thickness. It is heavily decorated with leather fringes, hanging plaques of abalone shell, and a virtual mosaic of tiny white clam shells. Some of the fringes have been wrapped with fine strips of the bear grass and maidenhair fern often used to embroider the excellent basketry of this region. The narrower front skirt is actually a piece of leather cut into long fringes, each strand completely wrapped with bear grass and trimmed with glass trade beads and olivella shells. Although the front skirt might be a solid piece of cloth or leather, it was invariably covered fully with some kind of decoration. The luxuriant ornamentation of these double skirts served as a form of religious exercise. Arrayed in this beautiful costume on ceremonial occasions, the Yurok woman embodied those qualities her people sought to emulate.

By the 1830's, native women in most parts of the western United States east of the Cascade-Sierras and west of the Mississippi were wearing simple leather binary dresses in two or three basic patterns. The simplest was made of two large animal skins whose natural shape was trimmed little or not at all. These were sewn together along the sides and at one end to make the shoulder seam, with openings left for the head and arms. This most basic of binary dress forms was worn primarily in the intermontane region, from the Jicarilla Apache of northern New Mexico to the Okanogan and their neighbors in southeastern British Columbia. It became the only leather dress worn consistently at any pueblo. The women of Taos, who presumably acquired the pattern from the neighboring Jicarilla and Ute, were wearing such garments regularly by the late 18th century. Taos binary dresses were trimmed somewhat to make square-cut cape sleeves and were decorated with yellow paint (cat. #94). Their lower edges were finished in a compound curve line that may have been derived from the shape of the animal skins themselves.

Although women of the northern Plains and Plateau occasionally wore such simple binary dresses heavily embellished with beadwork and other ornaments, they preferred a variant called the "deer tail" dress, which required two whole bighorn, mule

109 Worn by an initiate in the "Coming of Age" ceremony, this costume features a poncho and binary skirt. Chiricahua Apache, Arizona.

101

deer, or elk skins with the untrimmed tails left in place. The skins were joined in a straight line parallel to the rear edge, leaving an opening for the head. The excess leather to the rear of this seam, including the tails, was folded forward and tacked flat. When the sides were sewn closed and the dress was worn, the two tails appeared as ornaments at center chest and back. The undulating line of the skin's rear edge — what had been the animal's hind quarters and tail — now ran laterally across the upper part of the dress and became the basis for rows of quilled or beaded decoration (cat. #97). The front edges of the skins, originally a trifurcate shape caused by the projections of forelegs and neck, were filled in by the Plateau women to make full skirts with even bottom lines. Blackfeet women, on the other hand, retained and even emphasized the natural three-point bottom line with further decoration.

Another variant of the binary dress was made only by the Blackfeet and probably developed when available skins were not large enough to fold into the deer tail dress design. An extra piece was added at the top and the horizontal edges trimmed to approximate the flowing yoke lines of the deer tail dress. The decoration of these Blackfeet dresses also imitates that of the true deer tail dresses, making it difficult to tell them apart without a close examination.

What may have been the earliest kind of binary dress, the strap dress once worn from northeastern Canada west to the foothills of the northern Rockies, was noted by Alexander Mackenzie in western Canada as early as the 1790's. Made from two large pieces of leather trimmed into rectangles, sewn together along the sides, and supported by shoulder straps, this version of the binary dress covered the wearer from upper chest to mid-calf. Since it had a northerly distribution, the strap dress was often worn with separate leather sleeves (cat. #101). The use of these separate sleeves in a climate which would rarely require their removal is difficult to explain except in terms of the limited availability of hides large enough to permit the dress and sleeves to be cut, like the deer tail style, from two large skins. On the basis of the history of the strap dress, one might well theorize that Native American clothing styles changed in response to the introduction of the horse. The close relationship between the design of the binary dress and the shape of the animal skins from which it was cut suggests that the widespread popularity of the basic binary dress with a shoulder seam and the deer tail dress with its double thickness over the shoulders could not have occurred before the introduction of horses and firearms increased the ease with which large mammals were hunted and killed. The theory seems borne out by the fact that the deer tail dress style, which required two very large skins, replaced strap dresses among the Blackfeet, Crow, and other northern Plains women in the early 19th century, shortly after the horse and gun came into general use in the plains areas. Among the Woodlands tribes, however, where the horse never really became prevalent, strap dresses persisted even into the 20th century.

Until the 1870's, Navajo women wore simple binary dresses of handwoven woolen cloth (cat. #102). Although the Navajo probably learned weaving techniques from the Pueblo people in the 17th century, the idea of making binary dresses from cloth could not have come from their Pueblo neighbors, for no Pueblo woman has ever worn woven binary dresses. It has been suggested that the Navajos themselves had previously worn leather binary dresses and merely reinterpreted the concept in the new material. The Navajo woven dress illustrates an important principle of clothing design: decoration should be positioned for best effect. The Navajo weaver applied colored stripes or bands along the

94

top and bottom borders of the garment where they would not be particularly subject to folds, creases, or other visual distortion when the dress was worn.

When trade cloth was first introduced to the Plateau and Plains in the 19th century, native women continued to follow the binary leather dress styles with which they were familiar, but they soon learned that cloth had different working properties that required certain adjustments in construction. For one thing, cloth came in rolls of a uniform width that lacked the flaring contours of animal skins and handled best when cut or torn square. The Sioux child's dress illustrated here (cat. #105) shows how the leather dress form was adapted to the new material. The body was made of two rectangles just as the leather dresses had been, but additional cloth parts have been required to simulate the full contours of the animal skin. Two rectangular pieces have been added at the top to make the sleeve capes, and two long, triangular gussets have been sewn into the sides to give the skirt more width. These gussets extend a little below the bottom edge of the skirt and actually represent, in vestigial form, the forelegs of the animal skin from which the leather dress would have been made!

Late in the 19th century, the Crow of southern Montana developed an unusual kind of binary dress with long, closed sleeves. All other forms of binary dresses were sleeveless like the Navajo woven dress or had open cape sleeves like the deer tail dress. The innovative closed sleeve may well have been inspired by European garments, but the persistence of traditional modes is illustrated in the decoration of the closed-sleeve dress shown here (cat. #107). Although the garment itself is not cut in imitation of the older deer tail style popular with the Crow, its decorations are derived from the lateral rows of quillwork typical of the deer tail form. This late 19th century dress also shows a type of ornamentation peculiar to the Crow, who valued the upper canine teeth of elk for their decorative qualities. A dress lavishly trimmed with these "tushes" reportedly demonstrated the hunting prowess of its wearer's husband, for each elk has only two. Not surprisingly, the practical Crow frequently found it convenient to carve tushes in bone for use in clothing decoration.

The poncho — that familiar rectangle of material with a central opening for the head — was sometimes cut of one piece, sometimes of two pieces joined at the shoulders. Like many garments belonging to the folded clothing tradition, the one-piece poncho was implicitly binary in its conception, for it was made to be worn folded into two relatively equal parts designed to cover the front and back of the torso, just as leggings were folded to cover the front and back of the leg. The idea of joining two smaller, similarly shaped pieces of material along this natural fold line is actually the basis for the two-piece poncho and the binary dress. The poncho, whether folded or seamed into a front and back, has been included here in the binary tradition because in Native America it was almost always combined with other more truly binary forms.

102

105

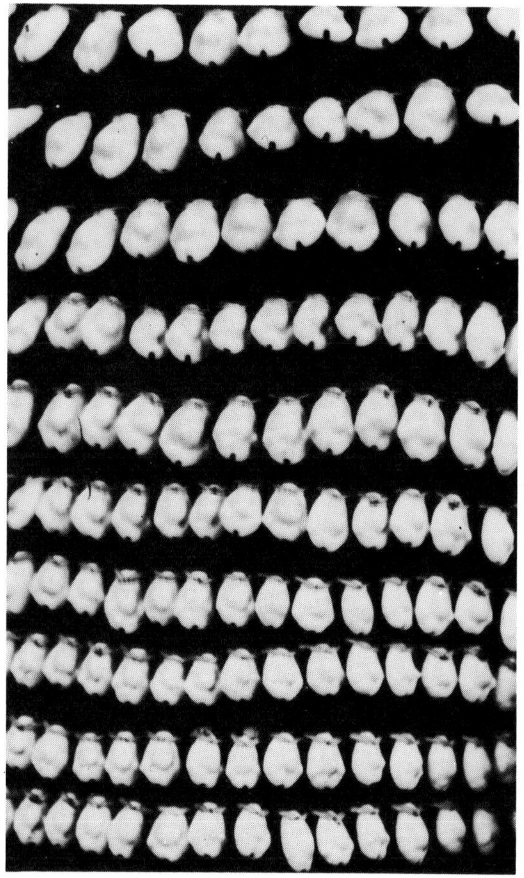

117

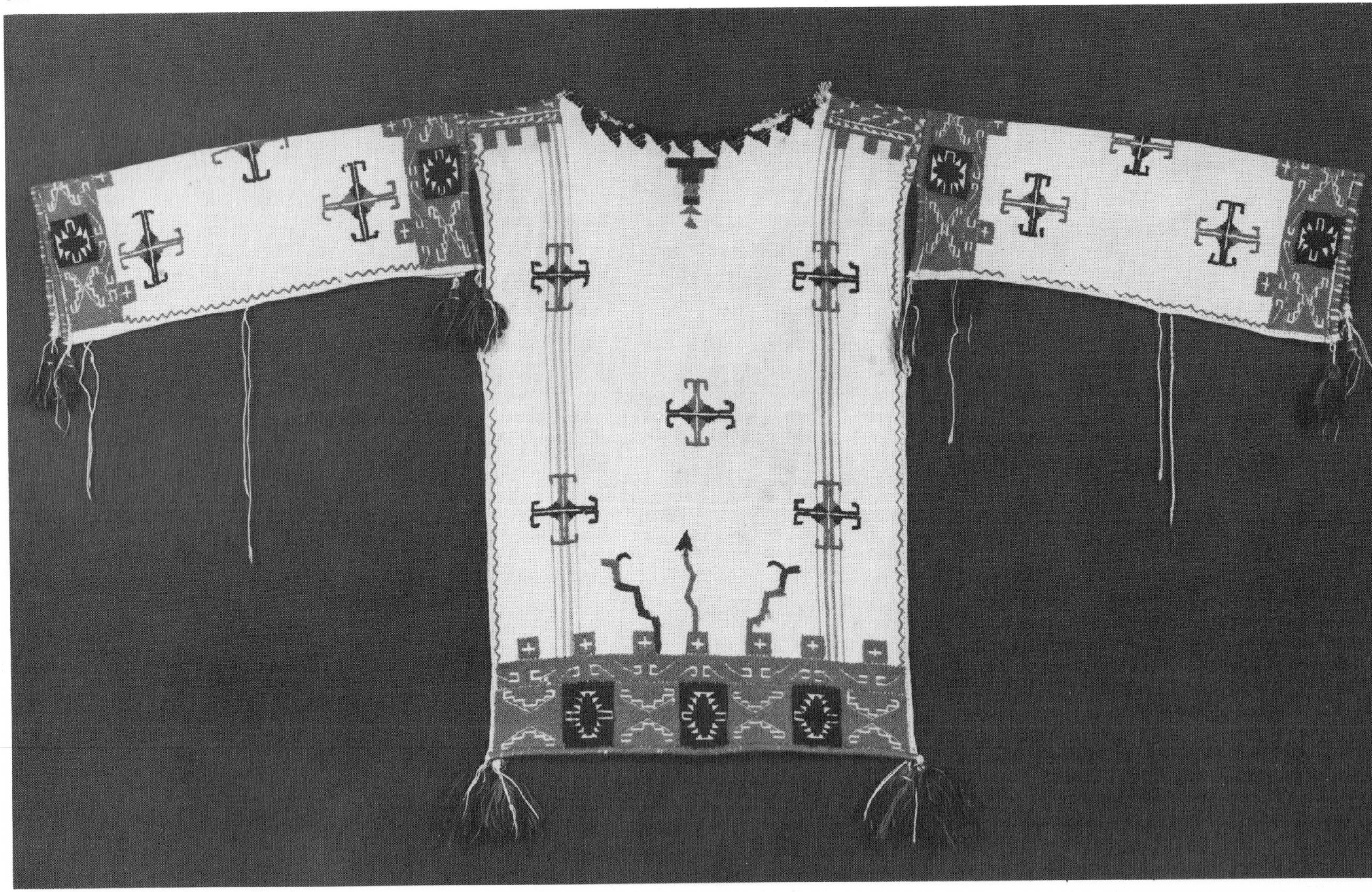

Apache women, for example, wore a combination of folded poncho and binary skirt as an everyday costume. One large deerskin with the four legs trimmed into decorative pendants at the corners served as the upper garment. A separate skirt, made of two medium-sized deerskins sewn up the sides, featured hind-leg pendants at the bottom edges. These dresses are worn today only for festival occasions. The example illustrated here (cat. #109) was made for a girl's coming-of-age ceremony and is resplendent with the conical tin "tinklers" esteemed as ornaments by the Apache because of their pleasing sound.

The dresses worn by women of the southern Plains tribes resemble the poncho-skirt combination of the Apache so closely that it is generally believed that the southern Plains tribes copied the style as early as the 18th century, modifying it into a one-piece garment by sewing the poncho directly to the skirt top. A ceremonial garment from the Pawnee Ghost Dance (cat. #111) illustrates both the style and the 19th century practice of painting leather clothing. The beautiful painting that covers the dress expresses the guiding vision of its owner, *i.e.,* the personal dream experience that was the basis for her participation in the dance. Today this custom of painting leather garments has virtually disappeared, but the southern Plains dress, usually of snow-white leather decorated lightly with beadwork, is still worn in western Oklahoma for such "dress" occasions as pageants, rodeos, and social dances.

Throughout most of North America south of the subarctic, native men wore binary shirts in various forms. Folded or seamed leather ponchos — sleeveless pullovers open at the sides — were worn by men through most of the eastern United States and sporadically in the west. On the northwest coast, 18th century chiefs' regalia included long ponchos of several sea otter pelts. Leaders of war parties in this area wore sealskin ponchos with the fur side in and the exposed smooth surface painted in the wearer's heraldic crests. In the southwest, Apache men made painted deerskin ponchos part of their ceremonial costume. Pueblo men, who wove and wore cotton and wool ponchos, sometimes added sleeves of rectangular pieces of cloth attached at the shoulders and left open at the sides. The Jemez shirt illustrated here (cat. #117) is native cotton cloth embroidered in hand-spun wool yarn by a unique method devised by the Pueblo people, but the Pueblo sleeved poncho is frequently made of dark wool cloth decorated only with ornamental weave.

Native America also produced several kinds of sleeved binary shirts. The basic type, worn as an everyday garment by men over most of the northern half of the continent, was very simple, with identical front and back pieces and sleeves shaped like equilateral trapezoids (cat. #118). Worn thin by the exertions of hunting and hard labor, comparatively few shirts of this type have survived, and it is usually the ornamental "dress" shirt variants that one sees in museums or in old photos.

One such variant, worn on the southern plains and parts of the adjacent intermontane region, was very close-fitting and decorated with unusually long, triangular neck flaps and long, fine fringes (cat. #121). Those from the southern Plains were lightly beaded or painted in solid colors, generally yellow. Those of the intermontane area, *i.e.,* Ute, Jicarilla Apache, Taos Pueblo, were seldom painted, but frequently beaded with wide shoulder bands in the manner of the central Plains.

The "deer leg" binary shirt of the central and northern Plains was originally worn as a mark of distinction by established warriors, civil leaders, and officers of military societies. The shirt required two large animal skins, each cut in two just behind the front legs. The back half of the skins became the body of the shirt with the hind legs left untrimmed

124

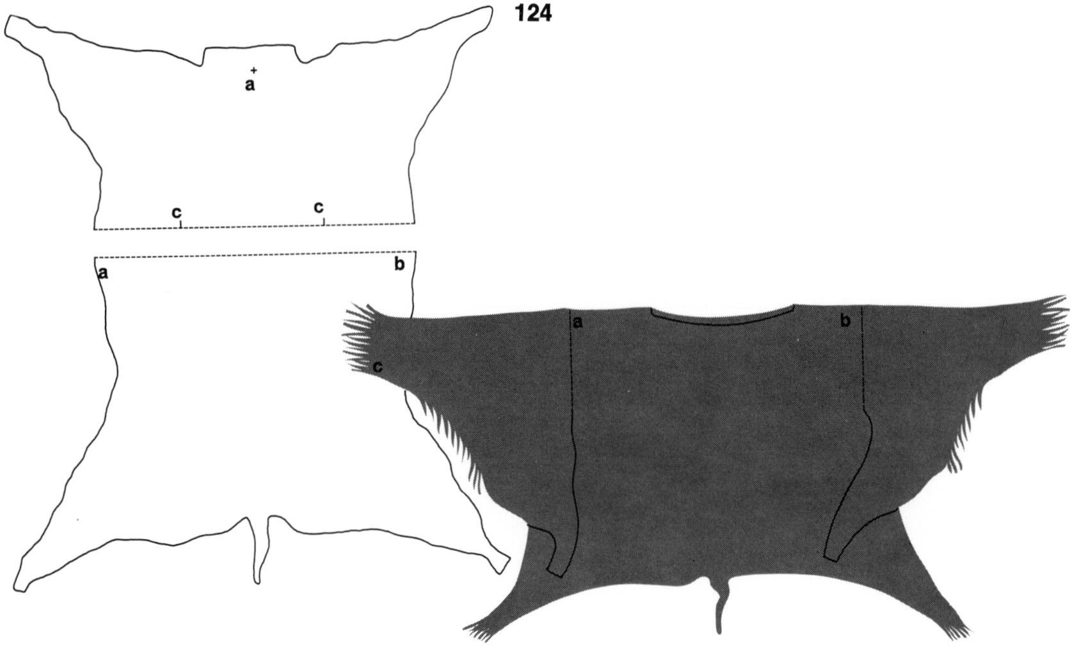

to dangle as decorative pendants at the bottom corners. The front halves were folded along the backbone line to make sleeves, with the forelegs retained as additional ornament. Decorative bands of quillwork or beadwork cascaded over the shoulders and down the sleeves. Deer leg shirts of the central Plains were further embellished with paint and long tassels of human hair symbolic of the wearer's battlefield exploits. Although these locks were once thought to have been cut from the heads of fallen enemies, they may have actually been gathered from family and friends. Deer leg shirts of the northern Plains and Plateau were occasionally painted and frequently decorated with hair locks or with long slender tubes of ermine skins (cat. #124). This elaborate shirt is still worn at times, but more often its decorations — hair locks, ermine tubes, and decorative bands — are applied to a square-cut binary shirt worn by Plains and Plateau men as a formal garment in parades or at native social events.

Although most Eskimo clothing falls into the advanced tradition of tailoring or fitting, pieced parkas worn in Alaska are closely related to the sleeved binary shirt. Strips of walrus intestine, cut open into long bands and cleaned, are sewn together to make waterproof parkas with straight-sided, rectangular bodies and sleeves (cat. #128). Birdskins trimmed into rectangular shapes are sometimes pieced together in a similar fashion (cat. #130). Little decoration is found on these utilitarian garments.

131

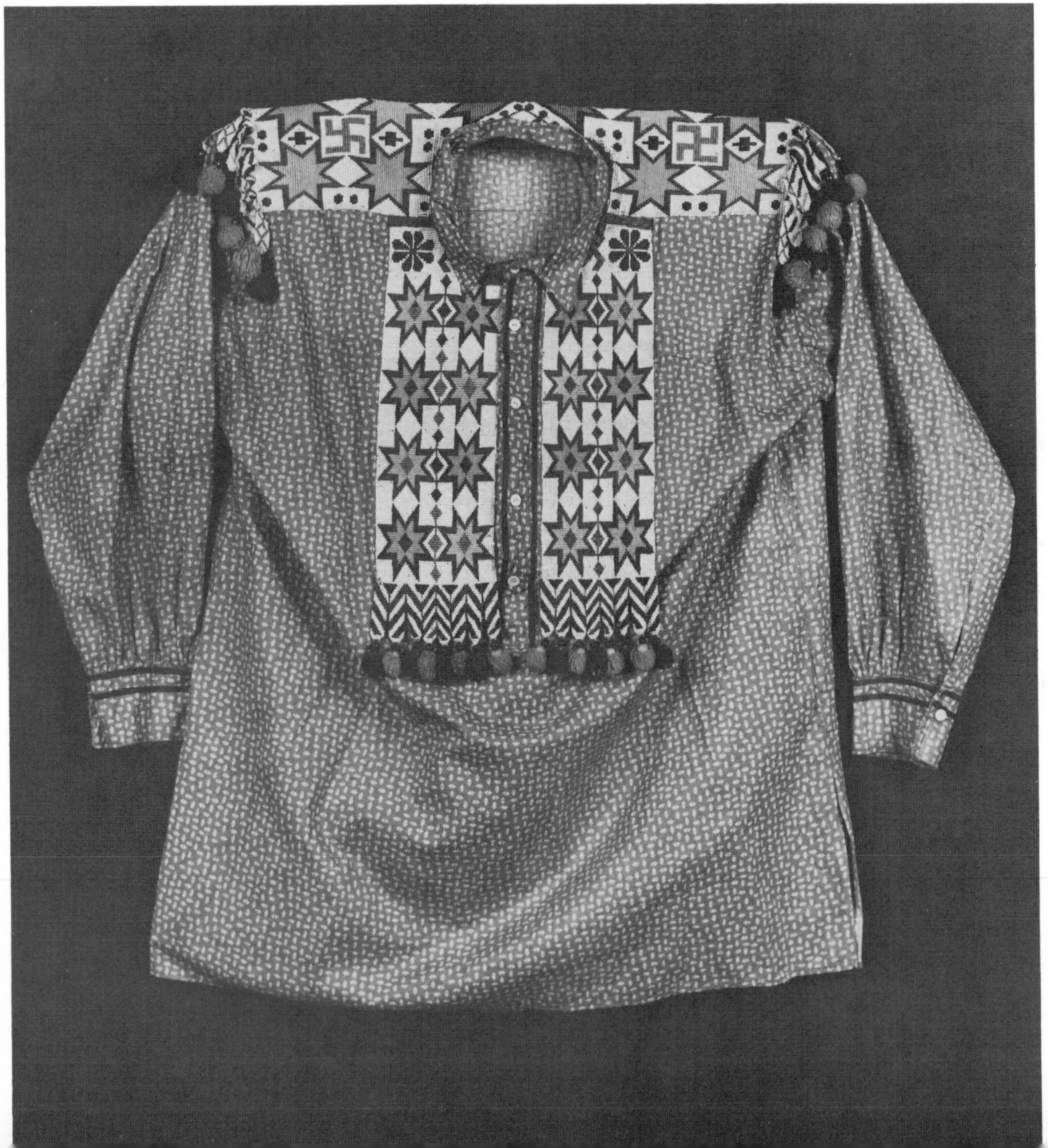

132

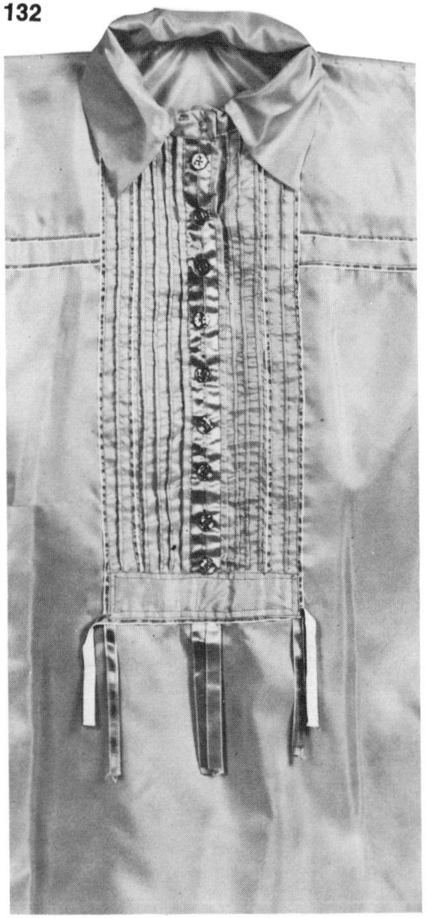

When muslin and other light trade cloth became available, simple binary shirts and blouses were made in these new materials. The "ribbon shirt" of Oklahoma and the midwest, which probably originated in the 18th century, is based on the rectangular pattern of the sleeved binary shirt with the European-inspired refinements of a vertical front opening and cuffed sleeves. In the late 19th century, men of the Great Lakes region added woven beadwork panels edged with bands of ribbon to the chests and shoulders of these shirts (cat. #131). Today in Oklahoma the beaded panels have been replaced by pleated chest panels and false yokes. The ribbon trim still stands, outlining areas once adorned with colorful beadwork (cat. #132). The modern ribbon shirt has found acceptance as part of contemporary dance costume through much of the west, and some young Native American men have adopted the garment as a symbol of pride in their ancestry.

As the ribbon shirt spread through the western Great Lakes and midwest, an analogous form came into use for women — a waist-length blouse of binary construction with rectangular sleeves gathered into cuffs. Among the Potawatomi and Delaware, full flounced collars inspired by the "berthas" of mid-Victorian European women became popular (cat. #134). Some groups, such as the Winnebago, often made blouses with no collar at all, and Ponca women sometimes cut theirs like that of the fashionable middy. Although the ribbon shirt and the blouse were made of European cloth and incorporated European ideas of clothing construction — gathering, separate cuffs, underarm gussets — their simple binary cut was not a European concept. Like other native garments, they maintained the basic principles of their construction despite the introduction of new materials and influences.

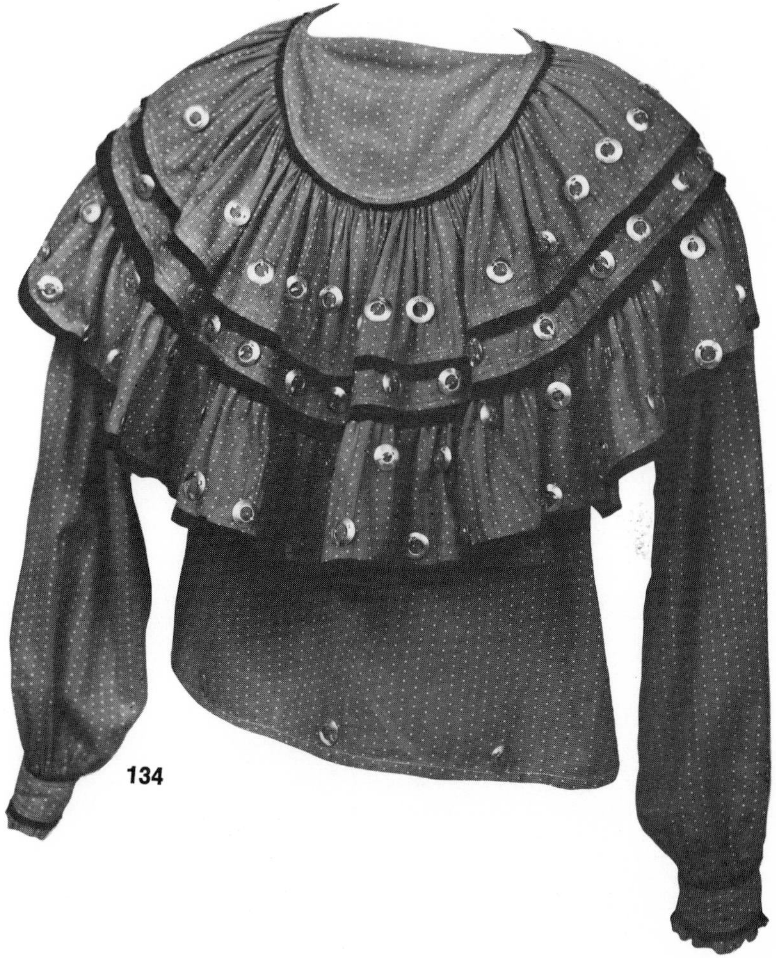

134

Binary Garments

•89
Double Aprons
Midwestern United States, late 19th century.
Beadwork on wool cloth, 20 x 18 in.
The beading shows the open, bilateral figures developed in the midwest in the late 19th century. Decorated aprons of this type were worn by men.
Denver Art Museum BCr-10

90
Double Aprons
Osage, Missouri and Oklahoma, 20th century.
Ribbon appliqué on velvet, 17 in.
A modern example of the double aprons worn with the Straight Dance costumes of the contemporary southern Plains.
Private Collection

•91
Fringe Skirts
Mojave, Southern California, c. 1860.
Willow bark and ravelled cloth, 28 x 31 in.
The ravelled trade cloth fringe is unusual since most fringe skirts from the west were made entirely of native materials.
Denver Art Museum CMo-2, RMo-1

92
Double Skirts
Yurok, Northern California, late 19th century.
Various native materials and trade beads on leather, back skirt 38 x 29 in., front skirt 15 x 21 in.
Highly decorated clothing of this type was worn for ceremonies designed to ensure the "Renewal of the World."
Denver Art Museum: Gift of Mrs. Donald Bromfield BYu-2, 4

93
Front Skirt
Karok, Northern California, late 19th century.
Trade beads and various native materials on cloth, 16½ x 29½ in.
Worn with a larger back skirt (see #92).
Denver Art Museum: Gift of Mrs. Donald Bromfield BKa-1

•pictured in catalog

•94
Binary Dress
Taos Pueblo, New Mexico, mid-19th century.
Painted leather, 45 in.
The square-cut sleeve capes, the undulating bottom line, and the areas painted in yellow are seen only on Taos dresses. The basic idea of the dress was probably introduced by the Jicarilla Apache or Ute, both of whom came to the pueblo to trade.
Denver Art Museum LTa-5

95
Binary Dress
Ute, Colorado and Utah, mid-19th century.
Painted leather with beads and trade cloth, 50 in.
Another example of the binary form popular in the intermontane area.
L. D. Bax Collection UTE 108

96
Deer Tail Dress
Nez Percé, Idaho, 1880's.
Pony Beads on leather, 50 in.
The example shows the deer tail at center chest and back and the decoration derived from the pattern.
L. D. Bax Collection PL 131

•97
Deer Tail Dress
Blackfeet, Alberta and Montana, late 19th century.
Beadwork on leather, 45½ in.
The undulating curve of the beadwork follows the lines of the natural material. The triangular cloth skirt ornament represents a buffalo head. This dress belonged to Coming Singing.
Denver Art Museum BBl-38

98
Deer Tail Dress
Blackfeet, Alberta and Montana, c. 1880.
Beadwork on leather, 53 in.
The deer tail may be seen at center chest and back.
Private Collection

99
Deer Tail Dress
Sioux, Dakotas, 1880's.
Beadwork on leather, 51 in.
The curving line of the deer tail pattern survives only in the beading. Heavily beaded dresses like this example were made late in the 19th century. The plumes indicate that the woman has participated in the Hunka, a ceremony honoring children.
Denver Art Museum BS-70

100
Strap Dress
Plains Cree, Saskatchewan, mid-19th century.
Painted leather, 45 in.
A typical example of the strap dress with matching separate sleeves. Collected by Isaac Cowie, a noted Episcopalian missionary, and exhibited at the World Columbian Exposition in 1893.
Field Museum of Natural History, Dept. of Anthropology 15005

•101
Strap Dress
Ojibwa, Western Great Lakes, 20th century.
Beadwork on leather, 47 in.
This is perhaps the last example made in this style. The strap dress is no longer worn.
Denver Art Museum BOj-54

•102
Binary Dress
Navajo, Arizona, 1860's.
Native wool cloth of natural and commercial yarns, 48 in.
A typical example of the dresses woven by Navajo women until the late 19th century. It consists of two rectangles joined along shoulders and sides.
Denver Art Museum: Gift of Alfred I. Barton RNd-21

103
Binary Dress
Navajo, Arizona, 1850's.
Native wool cloth, natural and commercial colors, 31 x 50 in.
Plain end stripes are the earliest known type of Navajo woven dress design. This is the only surviving example of the style.
Denver Art Museum RNd-10

111 The paintings and ornaments decorating the Ghost Dancer's costume are derived from visions. Pawnee, Nebraska and Oklahoma.

107

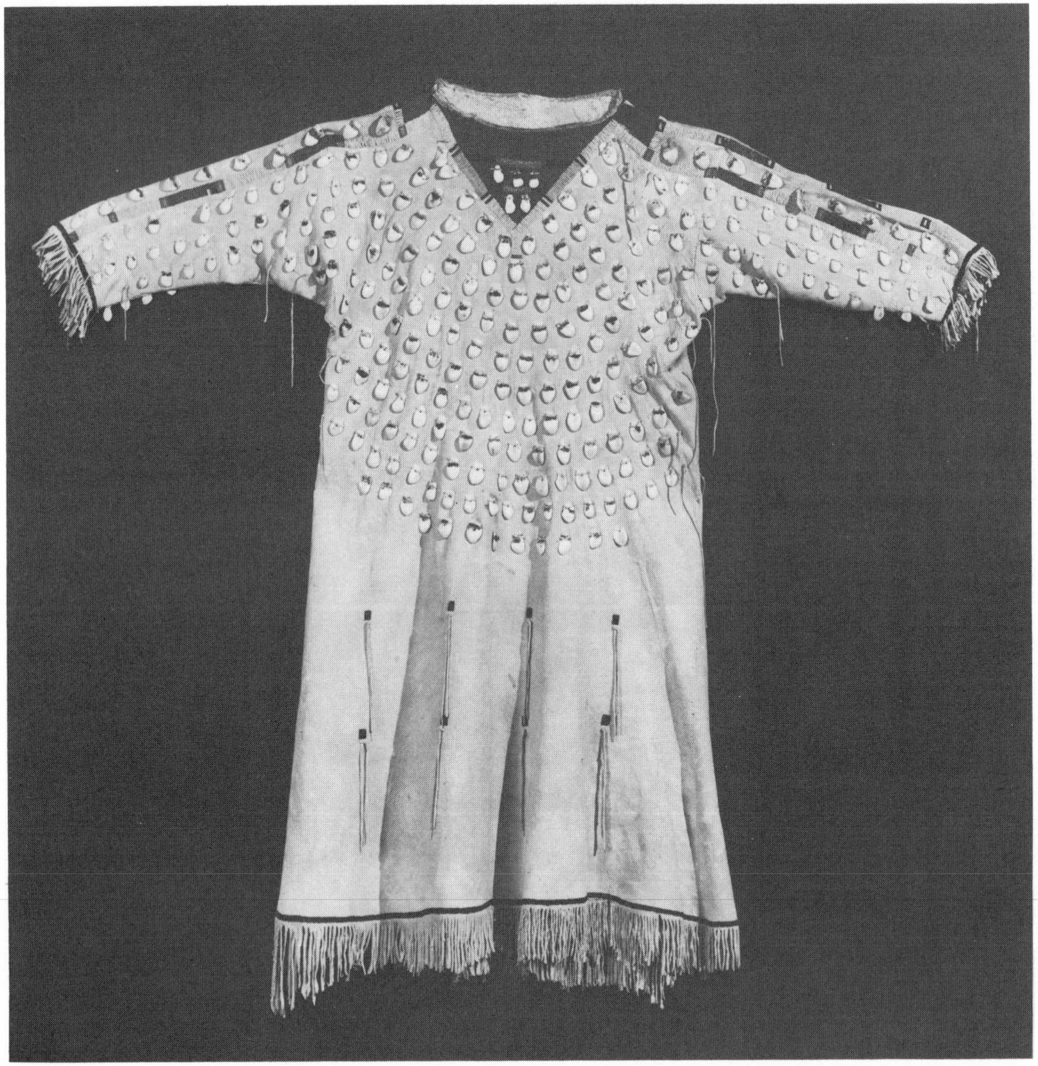

104
Binary Dress
Navajo, Arizona, c. 1890.
Native wool cloth, natural and commercial colors, 33½ x 53 in.
The terminal phase of Navajo woven dress design featured wide red end stripes with internal figures.
Denver Art Museum: Gift of Alfred I. Barton RNd-19

•105
Binary Dress
Sioux, Dakotas, 1870's.
Cowrie shells on strouding, 34 in.
An example of the binary concept in trade cloth with added sleeve pieces and gussets to give fullness to the skirt. The extensions of the gussets derive from the untrimmed forelegs used as decorative pendants in the leather form of this style.
Denver Art Museum BS-152

106
Binary Dress
Shoshone, Wyoming and Idaho, late 19th century.
Beadwork, cloth, and metallic fringe on strouding, 48½ in.
Another example of the binary form adjusted to trade cloth. Here the sleeves are partly closed.
Denver Art Museum: Gift of Mrs. Harry English BSs-14

•107
Binary Dress
Crow, Montana, early 20th century.
Beadwork, cloth, and carved bone ornaments on leather, 47 in.
Although the dress itself is cut in a simple binary pattern, its beaded decorations are derived from the earlier deer tail dress. Since the late 19th century, Crow leather and cloth dresses have had closed sleeves.
Denver Art Museum BCr-47

108
Binary Dress
Crow, Montana, late 19th century.
Beadwork and carved bone ornaments on strouding, 29 in.
A cloth example of the Crow binary dress with closed sleeves. The carved bone ornaments are imitations of elk tushes, upper canine teeth.
Denver Art Museum BCr-107

75

97

118

eather,

called
nt sound they

ed leather,

coming-of-age

netal ornaments, 55 in.
host Dance. The designs
al visions.
L. D. Bax Collec

112
Southern Plains Dress
Comanche, Oklahoma, 1870's.
Painted leather, beadwork and metal ornaments, 52½ in.
This simple painting shows the decoration favored for southern Plains clothing in pre-reservation times.
L. D. Bax Collection CO 109

113
Southern Plains Dress
Kiowa, Oklahoma, 1890's.
Painted leather, 53 in.
Like the Sioux, the southern Plains people held the Ghost Dance in the late 1880's, but theirs did not end in tragedy. The painting represents the wearer's personal visions.
Denver Art Museum LKi-8

114
Southern Plains Dress
Shoshone, Wyoming, late 19th century.
Beadwork and metal ornaments on leather, 54 in.
The style was probably copied from dresses worn by the neighboring Arapaho.
Denver Art Museum: Gift of F. H. Douglas BSs-16

115
Poncho
Hopi, Arizona, c. 1890.
Native wool cloth, handspun and raveled yarns, 24 x 72 in.
Collected at Keam's Canyon in 1895. Since Pueblo men's ponchos were often plain black or dark blue, these stripes are somewhat unusual.
Denver Art Museum RHc-37

116
Poncho
Ojibwa, Western Great Lakes, early 20th century.
Beaded trade cloth, 18 x 72 in.
This garment would normally be worn over a cloth shirt. The naturalistic floral designs are characteristic of Ojibwa beadwork.
Denver Art Museum BOj-28

•117
Binary Shirt
Jemez Pueblo, New Mexico, early 20th century.
Wool yarn embroidery on cotton sacking, 26 in.
The shirt has a simple binary body with added sleeves. The embroidery stitch was developed by the Pueblo people.
Denver Art Museum RJ-5

•118
Binary Shirt
Athabascan, Alaska, 1890's.
Beadwork and various ornaments on caribou leather, 42 in.
A simple form of binary shirt from an area that also produced more complex fitted clothing. See #144.
Lowie Museum of Anthropology, University of California, Berkeley 2-6708

119
Binary Shirt
Haida, Queen Charlotte Islands, British Columbia, late 19th century.
Appliqué of buttons and flannel on trade cloth, 34½ in.
The appliquéd figures represent the wearer's family crest, in this case a bear.
Denver Art Museum AHi-3

130

120
Binary Shirt
Blackfeet, Alberta and Montana, late 19th century.
Various ornaments on painted leather, 22 in.
The beaded horse and the shirt painting refer to the wearer's personal visions. Curley Bear, the owner of this shirt, was a functionary in the Sun Dance and may have worn this garment as part of his official regalia.
Denver Art Museum PBI-12

•121
Southern Plains Shirt
Arapaho, Oklahoma, early 20th century.
Leather, undecorated, 42 in.
This form of binary shirt, with long tight sleeves and fine fringes at elbows and shoulders, was made by the southern Plains and adjacent Intermontane groups.
Denver Art Museum LAr-19

122
Southern Plains Shirt
Jicarilla Apache, New Mexico, late 19th century.
Beadwork on leather, 21 in.
The Intermontane groups copied the southern Plains shirt form but added heavily beaded shoulder bands like those shown here. See #121.
Denver Art Museum BAJ-21

123
Southern Plains Shirt
Ute, Colorado and Utah, 1870's.
Beadwork and leather fringes on trade cloth, 26½ in.
An example of southern Plains pattern in cloth. The maker has added beaded shoulder bands and, since cloth will not fringe properly, leather fringes.
Denver Art Museum BU-26

•124
Deer Leg Shirt
Crow, Montana, late 19th century.
Beadwork and various ornaments on leather, 30 in.
Although collected among the Nez Percé, the garment is more likely Crow. The beaded shoulder and sleeve strips are typical of Plains shirts, and the ermine tube pendants are characteristic of the northern Plains and adjacent Plateau groups.
Denver Art Museum BNP-3

128

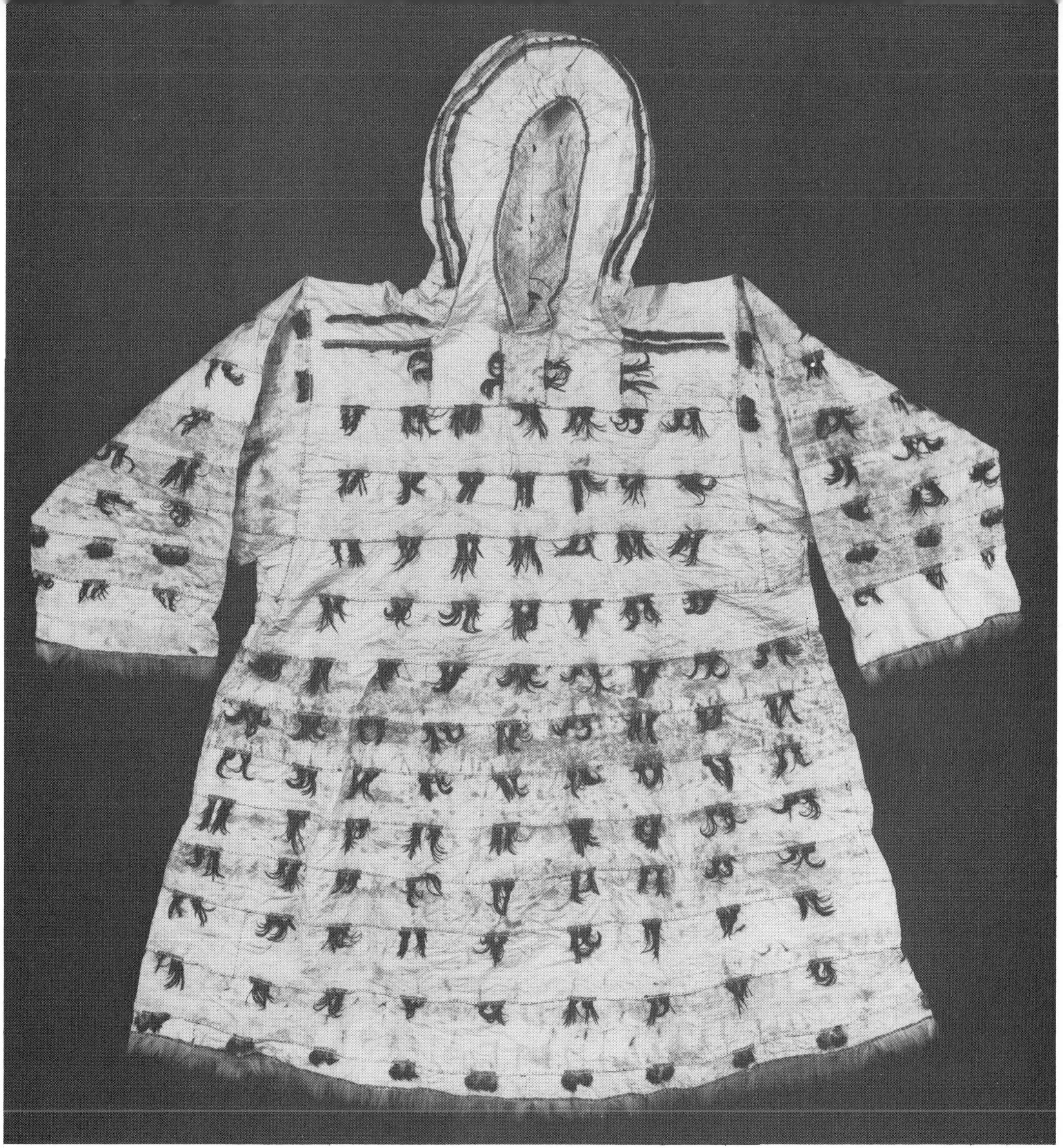

125
Deer Leg Shirt
Blackfeet, Alberta and Montana, 1880's.
Beadwork and ermine tube pendants on painted leather, 28½ in.
The painted spots are "wound" marks, indicating that the original owner had been wounded in intertribal warfare. Formerly in the collection of Joseph H. Sharp, the American painter.
Denver Art Museum BBI-64

126
Binary Shirt
Sioux, Dakotas, early 20th century.
Quillwork on leather, 31 in.
A good example of the shirts worn as formal clothing on plains reservations in this century. The shirt is cut on a simple binary pattern rather than the deer leg style formerly used for military shirts. Modern shirts, like this example, are usually unpainted.
Denver Art Museum VS-49

127
Deer Leg Shirt
Northeastern Oregon, mid-19th century.
Various ornaments on painted leather.
The rows of tiny holes derive from a vision and were supposed to render the wearer bulletproof in battle.
Field Museum of Natural History, Dept. of Anthropology 86492

•128
Binary Parka
Eskimo, St. Lawrence Island, Alaska, c. 1950.
Split walrus intestine with various ornaments, 48¼ in.
A waterproof garment worn by hunters in boats.
Denver Art Museum LEsk-7

129
Binary Parka
Eskimo, St. Lawrence Island, Alaska, c. 1940.
Split walrus intestine with various ornaments, 43 in.
Denver Art Museum 33-19-E

•130
Binary Parka
Eskimo, St. Lawrence Island, Alaska, 1940's.
Auklet skins and dog fur, 44 in.
Birdskin parkas were made only by Alaskan Eskimos. The skins have been trimmed into rectangles and sewn together to create this garment.
Denver Art Museum 30-19-E

•131
Binary Cloth Shirt
Potawatomi, Wisconsin and Kansas, late 19th century.
Woven beadwork panels and calico, 33 in.
An example of the 19th century light cloth shirt form incorporating beaded panels on chest and shoulders.
Denver Art Museum BPw-16

•132
Ribbon Shirt
Kickapoo, Mexico, 1972.
Rayon with ribbon trim, 36½ in.
A recent example of the binary cloth shirt. The beaded panels have been replaced with pleating, but the ribbons still outline the former position of the beadwork.
Denver Art Museum RKp-7

133
Binary Cloth Shirt
Ojibwa, Western Great Lakes, late 19th century.
Calico shirt with beaded velvet panels, 30½ in.
A variant of the midwestern cloth shirt with woven beadwork panels (see #131). The Ojibwa preferred dark clothing which set off their polychrome beadwork to advantage.
Denver Art Museum BOj-34

•134
Binary Blouse
Potawatomi, Wisconsin, mid-19th century.
Calico with ribbon trim and silver brooches, 18 in.
A simple binary pattern with gathered sleeves and a full "bertha" collar. The native-made brooches have been added as decorative elements.
Denver Art Museum JPw-28

135
Binary Blouse
Winnebago, Wisconsin, early 20th century.
Silk, cotton lining, 356 German silver brooches, 20 in.
The Winnebago often made simple blouses without collars. The brooches are native-made.
Denver Art Museum JWin-5

136
Binary Blouse
Ponca, Nebraska and Oklahoma, 1959.
Satin with ribbon trim, 21¼ in.
The square-cut back collar is a traditional Ponca style.
Denver Art Museum RPc-1

137
Binary Blouse
Potawatomi, Wisconsin and Kansas, early 20th century.
Beadwork on velvet, 21½ in.
From the Prairie Potawatomi of Kansas. The binary blouses of the Woodlands Potawatomi were cut like #134.
Denver Art Museum BPw-5

Fitted CLOTHING

Fitted Clothing

When people speak of a "tailored suit" or the "tailored look," they may have in mind any one of a number of specific definitions or general connotations. "Tailored" may denote methods of reinforcement intended to stiffen parts of some garment like the shoulders or jacket lapels, or it may refer to a garment made to order as opposed to one that is "ready-made." "Tailored" may also be used somewhat loosely to indicate a manner of styling — conjuring up vague visions of severe and unadorned suits for women.

Although students of Native American clothing have often applied the word "tailored" to garments made in the arctic and subarctic regions, none has ever defined the term in this context. Because all of our current definitions of tailoring are irrelevant or confusing when associated with these Native American garments, clothing usually described as "tailored" might more accurately be called "fitted." The fitted tradition of Native American clothing, quite naturally, includes garments meant to "fit" the human body closely rather than merely cover it. Because these garments are conceived three-dimensionally, they are constructed of many dissimilar pieces. Even the edges of adjoining parts, meant to be sewn together, are seldom straight or identical (cat. #148). The purpose of such intricate design is to insure the snug fit essential to existence in regions of extreme cold. Outside the arctic, native peoples found little need for fitted garments except footwear.

The simplest kind of fitted garment from Native America is the man's shirt from the Naskapi of Labrador, constructed of a one-piece back, two-piece front, two-piece sleeves, a collar, and gussets as needed, with most of the adjoining edges cut in opposing curves (cat. #138). Because of its similarities to certain garments in the European tradition, some observers have argued that the Naskapi shirt must have been derived from European models.

138 The collar and the extensive painted decoration of this fitted coat mark its wearer as a village leader. See pattern, p. 88. Naskapi, Labrador.

F. H. Douglas, however, has pointed out that the shirt is no more complex than a good many other garments made by the Naskapi and their neighbors. To his persuasive arguments in support of its being a native development, one might add that Native America can boast a good many fitted clothing forms far more complex than the Naskapi shirt and so unlike European clothing as to preclude any chance of outside influence.

In interior Alaska, at the opposite end of the North American subarctic, several groups of Athabascans formerly wore fitted leather shirts of a truly unique design. Instead of being seamed to the front at the top of the shoulder, the backs of these shirts fold forward diagonally to join the two front sections in seams running from the throat outward and down to the corners of the chest (cat. #144). Eskimo parkas also avoid true shoulder seams, but no other Native American shirts are cut like these Athabascan examples. Presumably, this unusual shoulder treatment was developed to provide a better fit and to avoid a seam in a stress area. Like this diagonal seam which conforms to the natural slope of the shoulder, the sleeves of the shirt reveal a sophisticated understanding of the body's structure and articulation: they were placed forward of the garment's median plane (like those of a modern suit) to accommodate the forward thrust of the human arm.

The principal ornament of the Athabascan shirt was a V-shaped band of porcupine quill or bead embroidery starting behind the shoulders and falling to a point at mid-chest. Since the decorative elements of Native American garments are usually placed in some relation to their construction, it is interesting to note that this band of embroidery is not. At most, it repeats the shirt's distinctive V-shaped bottom edge. It is possible that the ornament

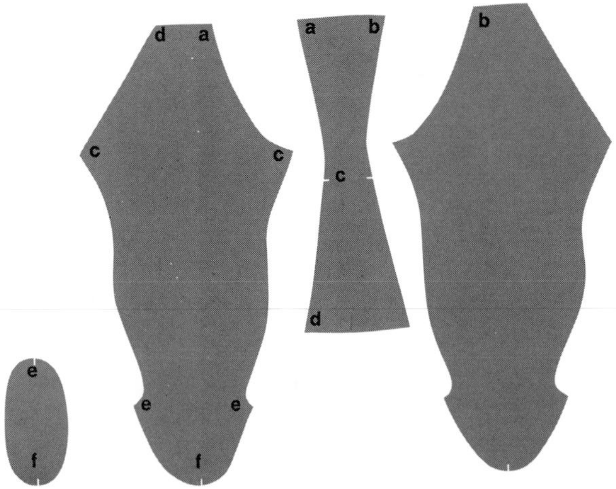

144

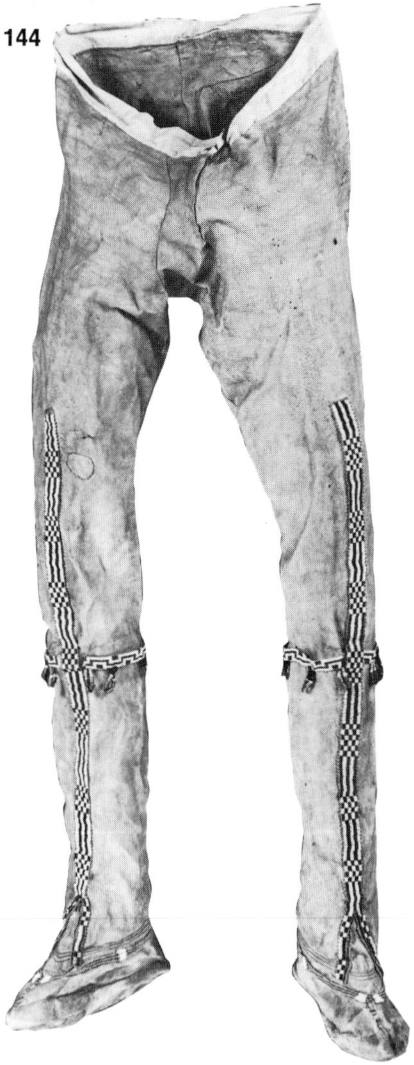

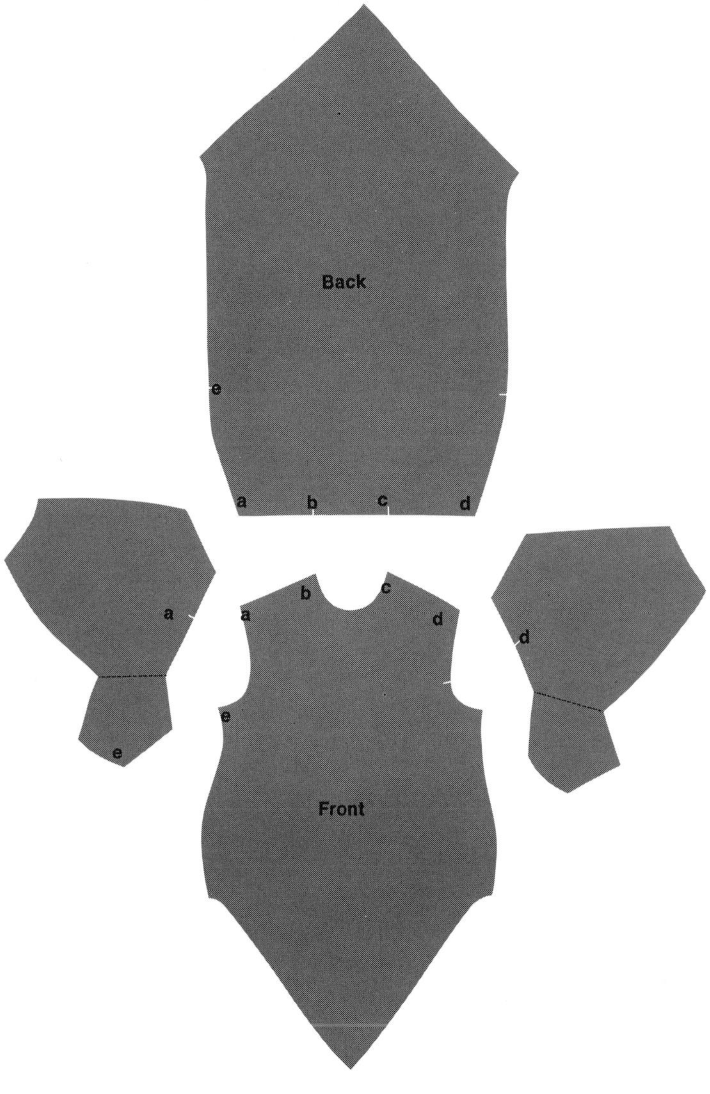

144

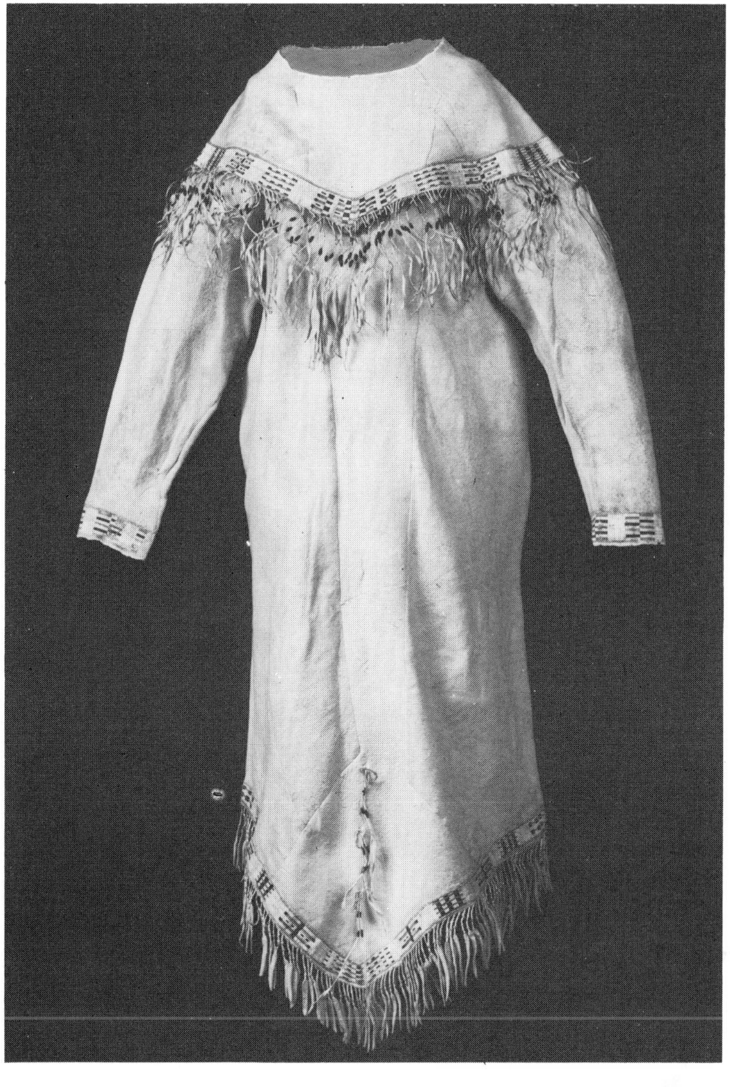

is a vestige of some earlier shirt pattern. Interestingly enough, the leather ponchos of the Athabascan-speaking Apache, who are thought to have once lived in central Canada, bear similar ornaments (cat. #109). Perhaps both shoulder decorations point to an earlier shirt pattern now forgotten.

With their remarkable pointed shirts, the Athabascan people wore such unusual lower garments that it is difficult to find a descriptive name for them. In general appearance these long, close-fitting trousers with feet most resemble the lower half of the modern day "sleeper" worn by young children. They were ingeniously constructed of one-piece legs, shoe soles, and a breechcloth-like piece to fill out the trunk area (cat. #144). Like the shirt pattern developed by the Athabascan people to guarantee the close fit required by their harsh environment, these trousers are seen nowhere else in North America.

A singular shirt from the Tanaina of the Kenai Peninsula epitomizes the northern genius for clothing design. Although this Athabascan garment was not available for exhibition, it is so remarkable that its pattern has been included (cat. #145). The whole shirt was cut in *one piece* from a large moose skin. By involved folding and cutting, a complex, three-dimensional garment was formed. To the best of our knowledge this garment is unique — surely in North America, and perhaps universally.

Among the various bands of Eskimos who live throughout the arctic from Greenland to East Cape in Siberia, both men and women wear fur clothing in ensembles of shirts (usually called by the Russian word "parka"), trousers, boots, and mittens. Within any Eskimo group, however, distinctive features characterize the clothing of each sex. For example, women's parkas are generally longer and often have a pouch-like swelling behind the shoulders for carrying an infant. Women usually wear thigh-length trousers and high boots while men wear knee-length trousers and shorter boots. Eskimo clothing varies regionally as well. The popular stereotype of the smiling Eskimo girl with her halo-like hood ruff of wolverine fur is valid only for certain parts of Alaska. Regional differences in details of cut and decoration become more pronounced as one moves from the Canadian arctic to Alaska or Greenland.

Taken as a group, however, Eskimo parkas share a common emphasis on good fit for comfort and survival. All are made from caribou and use the natural brown and white fur of these animals for warmth as well as decorative effect. All have been cut in many pieces and assembled into three-dimensional forms: their sleeves, for example, are designed to conform to the natural carriage of the human arm. True shoulder seams are avoided by extending the front or back sections over the top of the shoulders. This lowered seam placement provides more freedom of action by taking advantage of the caribou skin's natural elasticity at a place where much body movement begins. Since caribou skins are less durable than most animal leather, the life of the garment is also increased by placing these major seams in an area of reduced stress.

In order to get the precise fit they sought, the Eskimos used dressmaking devices uncommon in the rest of Native America. Among these are darts, gussets, and easing. Darts, which appear as small V-shaped cuts in several of the patterns, occur at places like sleeve cuffs and hood edges to reduce the diameter of an opening. Wedge-like or diamond-shaped gussets might be inserted at the tops of sleeves or in the "baby pockets" of women's parkas. Where lateral volume is needed, at an elbow for instance, one section is gathered slightly along the seam line and "eased" to another.

Eskimo clothing has traditionally been made in two sets: light inner garments with fur worn next to the body and heavy outer garments worn with fur exposed. Inner parkas, like most native undergarments,

145

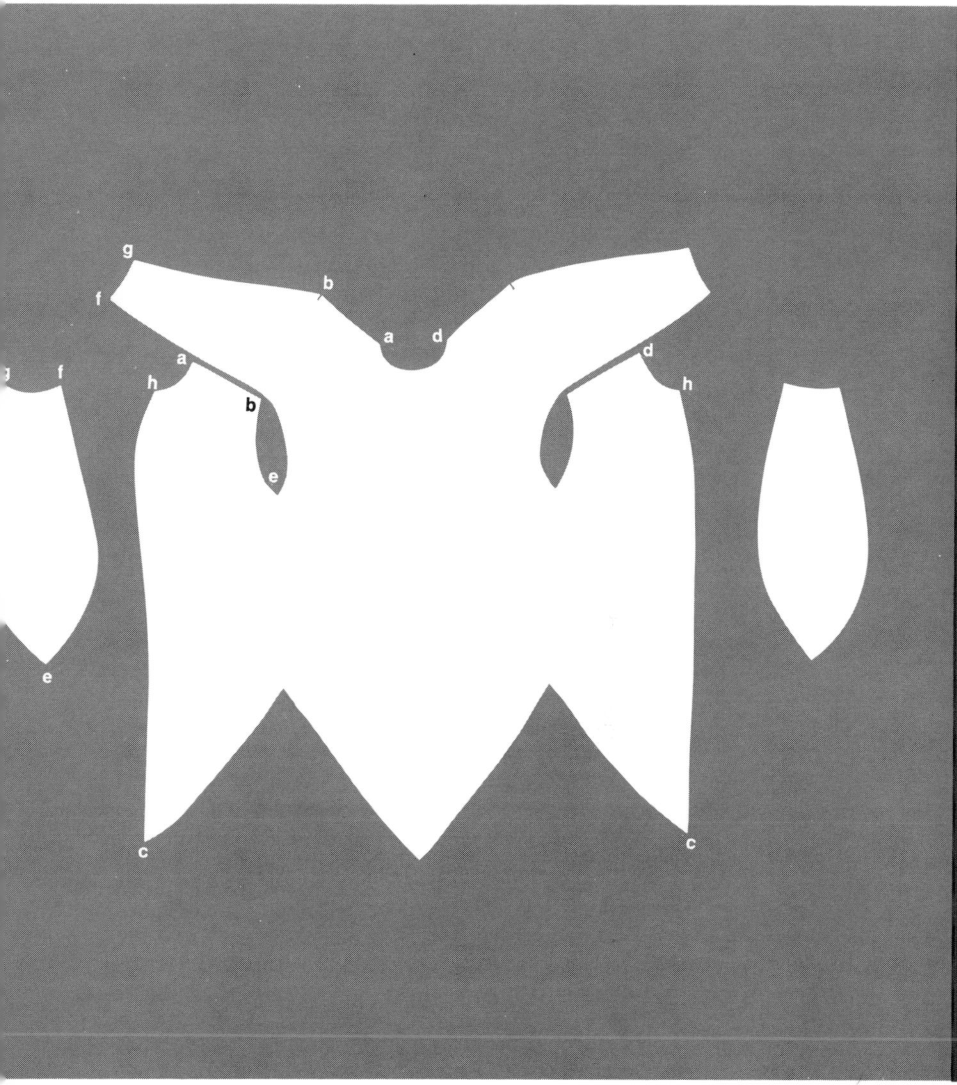

85

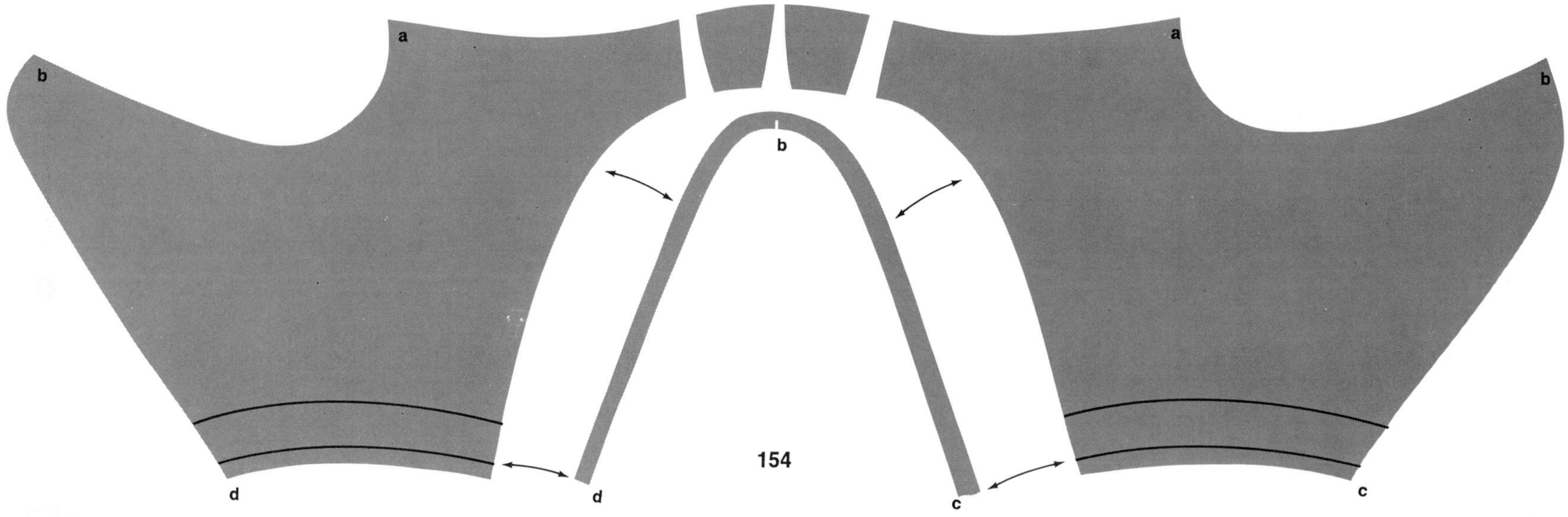

154

are usually undecorated. Outer parkas, constructed primarily of brown caribou fur are decorated with contrasting areas of natural white fur from the caribou belly. In Alaska, bits of bird down, yarn, and other colorful materials are often incorporated into the trim, which is usually limited to hoods and borders. However, some Alaskan parkas are easily identified by their unusual decorative throat gussets, two large white triangles of fur running from the hood base down onto the chest. Since 1920, Alaskan furwork has been characterized by a "fur mosaic" technique used to build up complicated geometric and animal figures, but these designs continue to be restricted to the border areas traditionally considered suitable for decoration (cat. #155). White fur has been used to greater ornamental advantage in the Canadian arctic where strips and patches of white are interpolated throughout the parka. Wide borders are sometimes built up of several strips of white fur or large areas of white inserted in decorative designs to break the monotony of large brown areas.

The fitted trousers worn by Eskimo men and women alike vary less in cut from region to region than parkas. In the central arctic, women's short trousers and the longer trousers worn by men are constructed of several pieces with an even waistline (cat. #148). In Alaska and Greenland, however, women wear trousers cut quite differently: each leg is made of one piece, and the waistline dips considerably in front (cat. #154). Trousers, like parkas, are decorated with borders of fur mosaic in Alaska, and the Copper Eskimo in particular favor deep trouser leg borders of fur mosaic or leather fringe.

Some years ago, Gudmund Hatt identified a basic distinction between Eskimo and other Native American footwear. The Eskimo boot, Hatt pointed out, is characterized by soles that cover both the bottom and sides of the feet without resorting to internal cuts or seams while the soles of other native footwear are cut to correspond exactly to the soles of the feet or are shaped by toe or heel seams. Hatt's conception of Eskimo footwear is exemplified in the pair of men's boots from Alaska (cat. #155.) Its elliptical rawhide sole covers the foot bottom and is bent up to surround the sides of the foot as well. Fine, even pleats are made at toe and heel to control the fullness and lift the sides into position before they are sewn to the fur upper. As the pattern shows, no cut or seam has been made within the sole's circumference.

This basic Eskimo shoe was worn in Alaska and Greenland year around, but only in spring and summer in the central arctic. Here a slipper-like rawhide shoe was worn over two pairs of fur stockings in seasons of extreme cold. The slipper is shaped from one main piece which covers both sole and instep up to the ankle. Again the fullness is controlled by long, neat pleating, and no cuts or seams are used to form either toe or heel. The most remarkable examples of Arctic footwear are the long, full boots worn by central Eskimo women. Conventional in other respects, these boots incorporate a pouch-like and apparently non-functional lateral projection at knee level (cat. #148). Various explanations, most of them far-fetched, have been advanced for this remarkable design, but the best assumption seems to be that the pouch once served some long-forgotten purpose.

South of the arctic, most Native Americans wore some kind of fitted leather shoes. Usually referred to by the Algonquian word "moccasins," these fitted garments were intended to conform "like a second skin." Since "soft sole" moccasins made of soft-tanned leather were typical of forested areas and "hard sole" moccasins were worn in the drier and more barren southwest and plains, moccasins offer another example of clothing forms influenced by environment.

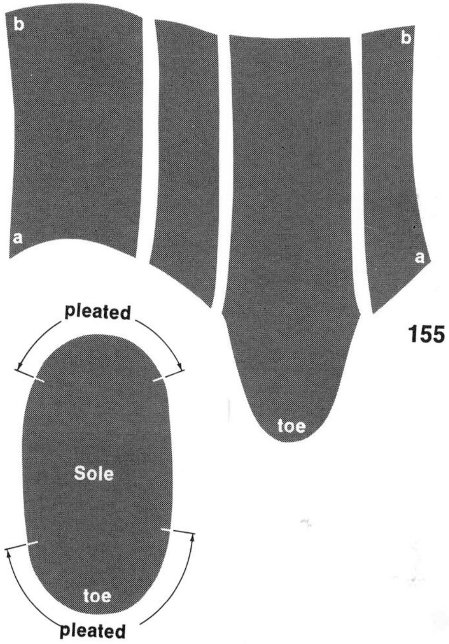

155

a
a
a
b
b
b
b
c
c

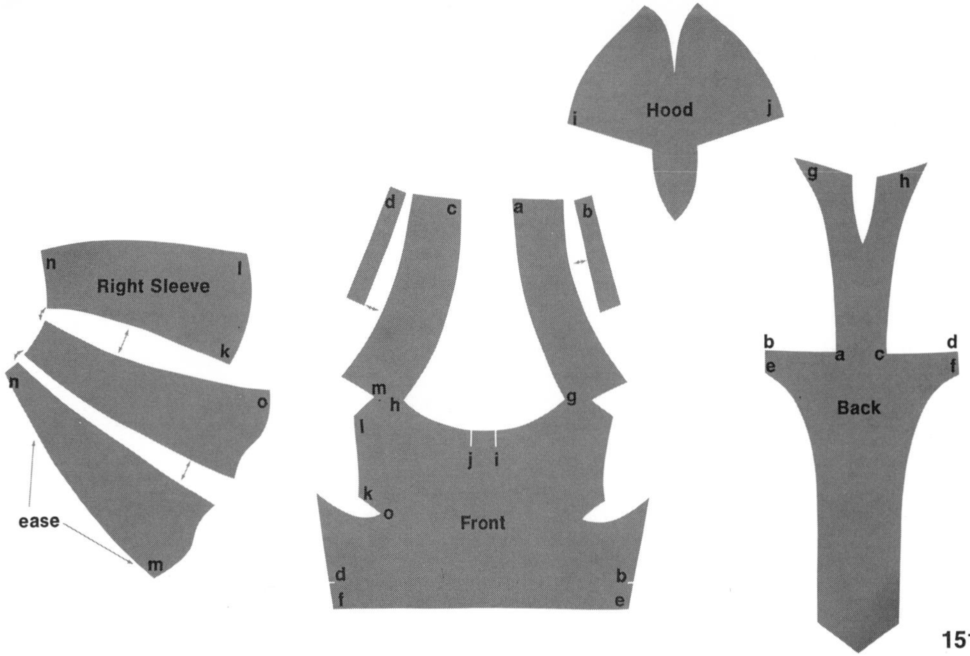
Hood
i
j
Right Sleeve
n
l
k
n
o
ease
m
d
c
a
b
m
h
g
l
j
i
k
o
Front
d
f
b
e
g
h
b
a
c
d
e
f
Back

151

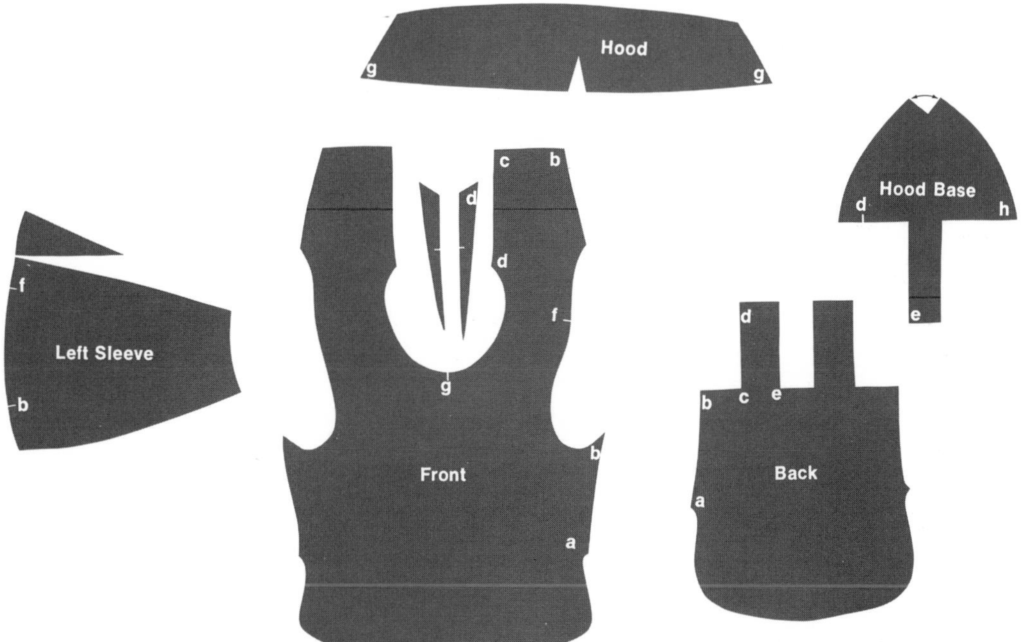
Hood
g
g
Hood Base
d
h
e
c
b
d
d
f
g
Left Sleeve
f
b
Front
b
a
d
b
c
e
Back
a

149

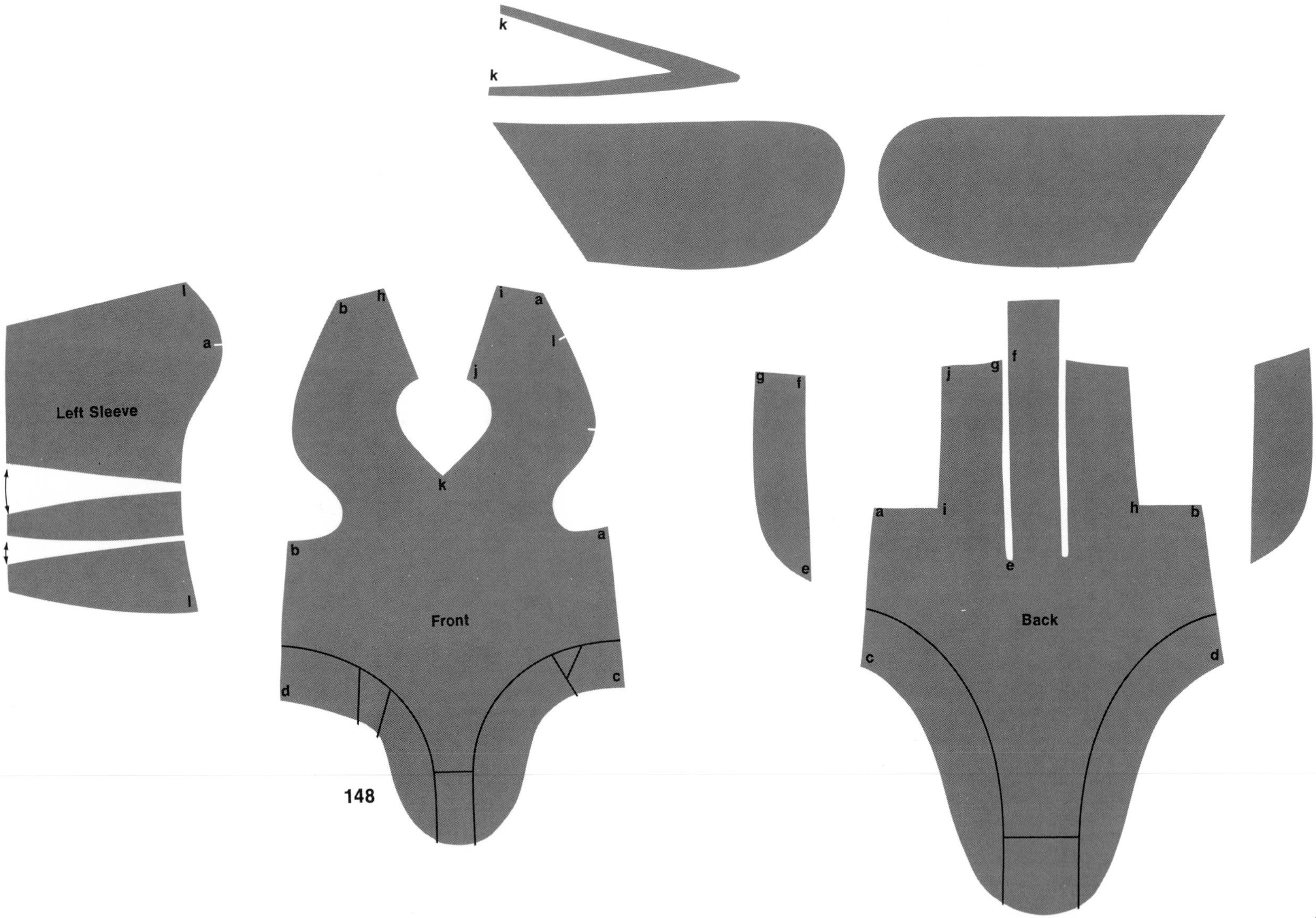

148

148

One type of soft sole moccasin, worn throughout the subarctic and northeastern quarter of the United States, is similar to the Eskimo boot in its turned-up sole. Unlike the true arctic shoe, however, the sole of this moccasin always has at least one internal cut and a seam shaping the heel. In this pattern, which we have called "Soft Sole I" here, the sole is turned up over the foot and gathered — never pleated like the Eskimo boot — to a U-shaped instep piece. The sole sides and heel are sewn, without gathering, to a counter rising to the ankle. Decoration is invariably placed on the instep, where the designs used for ornamentation are influenced by its "U" shape (cat. #158).

A closely related moccasin (Soft Sole II) is found over most of the eastern and midwestern United States, with the handsomest examples coming from the tribes of the southern Great Lakes and Ohio River valley. In this pattern, the instep piece has been eliminated, and the sole edges are gathered over the instep in a seam running from toe to ankle. Although this gathered toe seam flattens out somewhat in use, the instep area is still uneven enough to make decoration difficult. Thus, many moccasins cut in this pattern are characterized by wide ankle flaps whose only purpose seems to be decorative (cat. #166).

The hard sole Plains moccasin which has spread in recent times to most of the western United States is such a familiar part of the Native American stereotype that, in the minds of many, it is the only *bona fide* native shoe. It consists of a flat rawhide sole cut to approximate the shape of the bottom of the foot and a one-piece fitted upper of soft leather. A tongue and ankle flap may be added. This basic Plains moccasin, Hard Sole I, was once the standard native man's shoe from Texas to Alberta (cat. #172). With subtle differences, the same moccasin was worn by women of the north and central Plains, who

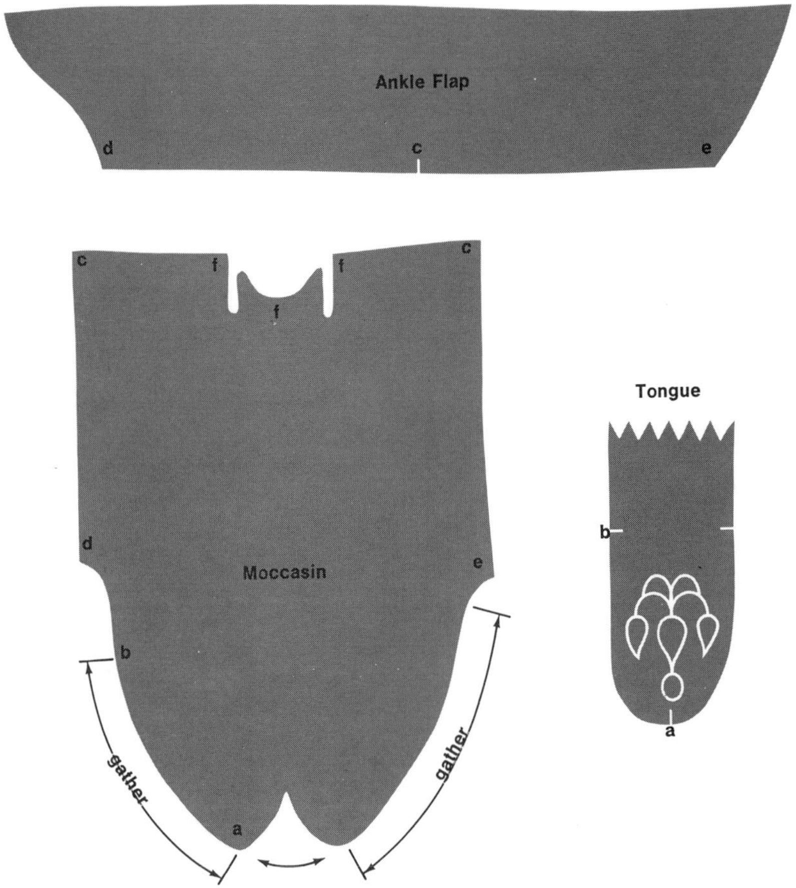

158

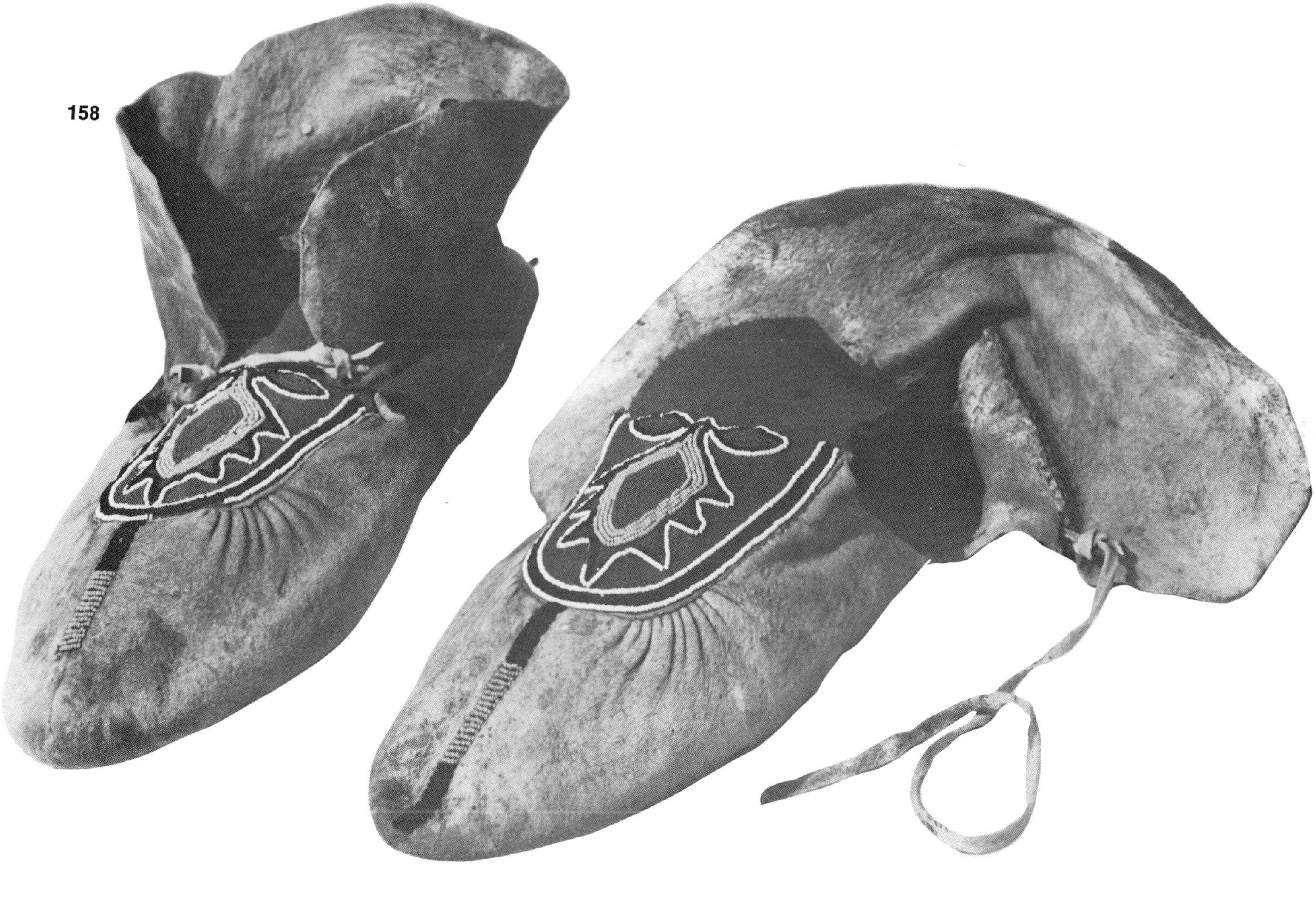

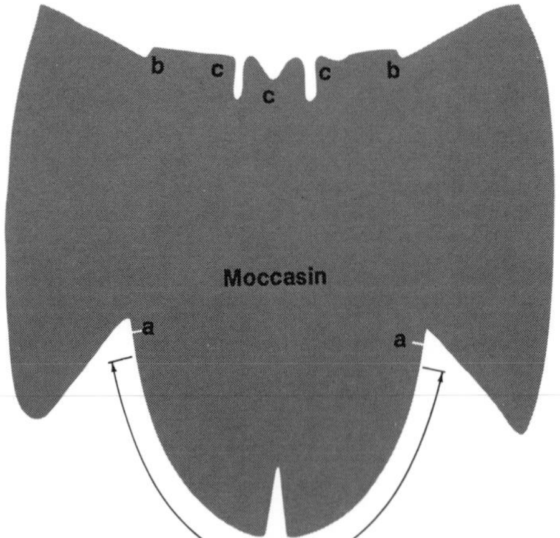

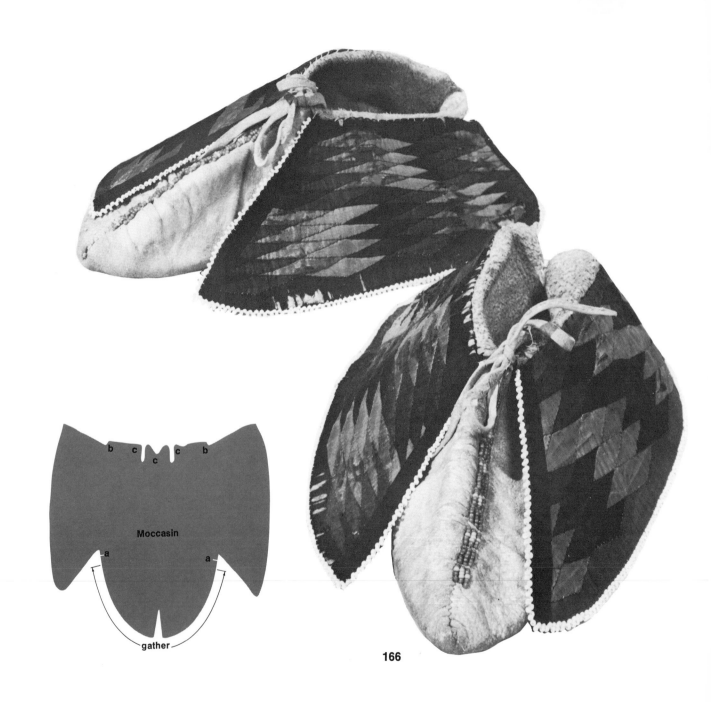

b
c
c
c
b
Moccasin
a
a
gather

combined it with separate leggings, and southern Plains women who sewed their moccasins directly to knee-high leggings (cat. #193). From the basic Plains hard sole form, a number of distinctive tribal moccasin styles have developed characterized by minor variations in cut and more obvious differences in decorative materials — painted designs, fringes, quill and beadwork, metal "tinklers," and silver ornaments.

Made in the southwest by the Navajo and most Pueblo groups, a second type of hard sole moccasin consists of a rawhide sole that curves slightly around the foot and a soft upper of one or more pieces that rises above the ankle. This upper may be left open along one side and fastened with tie strings or silver buttons, or it may be closed and extended into several boot-like forms. It has sometimes been assumed that the curved rawhide soles are shaped over wooden forms. In fact, the soles take on their curving configuration as a natural consequence of the sewing method and subsequent wear and handling. Moccasins of this kind are usually decorated only with dye or paint. The Navajo stain the uppers of theirs a reddish brown with mountain mahogany, leave the soles natural, and sometimes add silver buttons as side fastenings (cat. #197). The Pueblo people frequently dye men's everyday shoes in this manner, but women's shoes and men's ceremonial boots more often feature black soles and white uppers. Some of the masked dancers who impersonate kachinas wear short boots in this style decorated with conventional designs in several colors (cat. #205).

Worn by certain Apache groups, Hard Sole III is actually a variation of the Navajo-Pueblo style and is distinguished by several unusual toe forms ranging from the pointed toes favored by the Jicarilla (cat. #207) to the circular projections of western Apache shoes (cat. #206). Several fanciful explanations have been advanced for these toe forms, including one conjecture that the upturned toe prevents rattlesnake bites! The best suggestion so far points out the resemblance between the Apache shoes and some 16th and 17th century Spanish boot forms. The Apaches cut their distinctive shoes as ankle-high moccasins and as knee-length boots, sometimes with several deep folds that might be drawn up to cover the knees and lower thighs for walking in the areas of chaparral and cacti that abound in Apache country.

Although most of us are aware of the ingenuity and creative ability of the Native American, few realize how these skills have been demonstrated in clothing design and decoration. The examples of fitted clothing described here show how great these skills actually were. The Eskimo parka and Athabascan shirt rank among the most beautiful and imaginative garments ever devised.

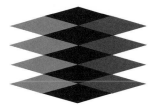

Fitted Garments

•138
Naskapi Shirt
Naskapi, Labrador, c. 1920.
Painted caribou skins, 39 in.
The extensive painting and the collar indicate a man of well-to-do or chiefly status. The accompanying pattern shows the cut.
Denver Art Museum PNs-7

139
Naskapi Shirt
Naskapi, Labrador, late 18th century.
Painted caribou skins, 39½ in.
A rare early example of northeastern clothing. Formerly in the collection of Sir Henry Wellcome.
Denver Art Museum PNs-56

140
Naskapi Shirt
Naskapi, Labrador, c. 1920.
Painted caribou skins, 40 in.
A man's winter shirt with fur worn inside. The bead pendants are charms to bring luck in hunting.
Denver Art Museum PNs-43

141
Belt
Naskapi, Labrador, c. 1920.
Painted caribou skin, 45¼ in.
Worn with shirts in winter. This belt has been included as an example of Naskapi leather painting.
Denver Art Museum PNs-3

142
Purse
Naskapi, Labrador, c. 1920.
Painted caribou skin, 14 in.
Included as an example of Naskapi leather painting. The bold designs were painted with native and trade pigments ground into a medium of water and the dried roe of the suckerfish. In use the purse is rolled and tied.
Denver Art Museum PNs-45

143
Athabascan Shirt
Kutchin, Interior Alaska and Yukon, mid-19th century.
Quillwork and beads on leather, 50½ in.
Made according to the pattern of #144. See text for comments on the design and decoration.
Denver Art Museum LKu-1

•144
Athabascan Shirt and Trousers
Athabascan, Alaska, late 19th century.
Leather with beadwork, quillwork, and various ornaments.
The characteristic suit worn by men and women alike. The cut is shown by the pattern diagram. Because these shirts and trousers were often conceived as an "outfit," they were frequently embroidered in bands of matching decoration.
Lowie Museum of Anthropology, University of California, Berkeley 2-19045, 2-6722

•145
Athabascan Shirt
Tanaina, Cook's Inlet, Alaska, late 19th century.
Dentalia shells, quillwork, and beadwork on leather, 53 in.
A unique garment, with body and sleeves cut in one piece. See accompanying pattern.
Collected by James G. Swan in the 1890's.
Thomas Burke Memorial Washington State Museum 145
Photo courtesy of the Washington State Museum

•146
Alaskan Eskimo Woman's Parka
Unalakleet, Alaska, 20th century.
Reindeer skins, wolverine fur ruff, various decorative materials, 52½ in.
The hood ruff is uniquely Alaskan, and the deep bottom flaps are peculiar to women's parkas. The cut is shown by the accompanying pattern.
Denver Art Museum 115-23-E

•147
Alaskan Eskimo Man's Parka
Western Alaska, 20th century.
Caribou skins, 46 in.
An undecorated parka for daily use. The cut is shown in the accompanying pattern.
Denver Art Museum 101-19-E

•148
Caribou Eskimo Woman's Suit
Caribou Eskimo, Keewatin Territory, Canada, 20th century.
Caribou leather and fur.
The elongated hood is worn only by women and is unique to this central Eskimo group. Note the striking effect achieved by inserting panels of white belly fur into the dark brown garment. The unusual cut of the boots is explained by the accompanying diagram. The parka illustrates the nature of a fitted garment. The front and back pieces, like the sections of the sleeve, are not the same approximate shape, as they are in binary garments. Several opposing curves that will be joined in seams have been marked on the pattern. The small letters show how the various pieces will be joined into the complicated garment.
Parka and trousers: Manitoba Museum of Man and Nature, Winnipeg, Canada H5.21-409, H5.21-390
Boots: Collection of the late Bishop Donald B. Marsh at the Manitoba Museum of Man and Nature H5.21-375

•149
Caribou Eskimo Man's Suit
Caribou Eskimo, Keewatin Territory, Canada, 20th century.
Caribou leather and fur with beaded cloth panels.
A summer costume. The central Eskimo people have more frequent contacts with Indian groups than their counterparts in Greenland or Alaska do. From the Indians they have borrowed the use of beadwork to decorate clothing.
Parka, stockings, and trousers: Collection of the late Bishop Donald B. Marsh at the Manitoba Museum of Man and Nature, Winnipeg, Canada H5.21-291, H5.21-113, H5.21-374
Mittens and Shoes: Manitoba Museum of Man and Nature H5.21-399, H5.21-405

•150
Copper Eskimo Woman's Suit
Northwest Territories, Canada, early 20th century.
Caribou furs.
The cut is shown by the accompanying patterns.
National Museum of Man of Canada, Division of Ethnology IV-C-584, 1744, 1745, 2983

•151
Copper Eskimo Man's Suit
Northwest Territories, Canada, early 20th century.
Caribou furs.
The accompanying pattern diagrams show how these garments were assembled.
National Museum of Man of Canada, Division of Ethnology IV-C-664, 1746, 1747, 1750

•pictured in catalog

173

152
Caribou Eskimo Man's Inner Parka
Caribou Eskimo, Keewatin Territory, Canada, 20th century.
Caribou fur with cloth tape trim.
A shaman's parka, worn while curing the sick. The unusual appliqués of red cloth binding were associated with the owner's profession.
Collection of the late Bishop Donald B. Marsh at the Manitoba Museum of Man and Nature, Winnipeg, Canada H5.21-155

153
Mackenzie Eskimo Woman's Parka
Coppermine River, Northwest Territories, Canada, 1947.
Caribou skins, 34 in.
A recent example of fur mosaic, showing both large body inserts and finer border figures.
Denver Art Museum: Gift of William C. Schnitzler FEsk-7

•154
Alaskan Eskimo Woman's Trousers
St. Lawrence Island, Alaska, 1940's.
Hair seal and reindeer skins, various ornaments, 15 in.
Short trousers were worn in combination with long boots at the east and west ends of Eskimo territory. The cut is shown by the accompanying pattern.
Denver Art Museum 98-19-E

•155
Alaskan Eskimo Man's Boots
Aniak, Alaska, 1940's.
Beard seal soles, uppers of caribou, wolverine, and various skins with cloth and yarn trim, 17½ in.
The decorative band around the top is an example of "fur mosaic." The fine pleating of the soles at toe and heel is common to most Arctic footwear. The accompanying pattern shows how the boots were cut.
Denver Art Museum 120-25-E

156
Mackenzie Eskimo Woman's Boots
Coppermine River, Northwest Territories, Canada, 1947.
Sealskin soles, caribou skin uppers with cloth trim, 10 in.
Made like #155.
Denver Art Museum: Gift of William C. Schnitzler FEsk-8

157
Alaskan Eskimo Man's Boots
Western Alaska, 1940's.
Beard seal soles, spotted seal uppers, 16½ in.
Made for winter wear. A maritime people, the Alaskan Eskimos have developed sewing techniques that produce waterproof seams.
Denver Art Museum 95-19-E

•158
Soft Sole Moccasins
Plains Cree, Saskatchewan, 1860's.
Beadwork and beaded cloth on leather, 10½ in.
An example of Soft Sole I pattern with both toe and heel seams. The decorated cloth panel corresponds to the underlying leather instep piece, as shown by the accompanying pattern.
Denver Art Museum BPiC-2

159
Soft Sole Moccasins
Northeastern Plains, 1830's.
Silk ribbon appliqué and quillwork on leather, 7¾ in.
Another example of Soft Sole I pattern (see #158).
Denver Art Museum APiC-1

160
Soft Sole Moccasins
Naskapi, Labrador, c. 1920.
Painted leather, 20½ in.
The Naskapi are said to have worn long footed trousers like those made by the Alaskan Athabascans until sometime in the 1880s, but there are no surviving examples. Since then Naskapi men have worn leggings and high moccasin-boots like this pair, another example of Soft Sole I pattern (see #158). Naskapi design is noted for its bold painted decoration. The "double curve" figure seen in native art over most of Canada and the northern United States is at its purest among the Naskapi. The motif consists of two equal curving lines arising in mirror opposition from a common center.
Denver Art Museum PNs-20

161
Soft Sole Moccasins
Ojibwa, Western Great Lakes, early 20th century.
Beaded velvet on leather, 10½ in.
The Ojibwa have long favored dark garments with light-colored embroidery. In the mid-19th century they began to make extensive use of dark velvet. Another example of Soft Sole I pattern (see #158). Collected by S. A. Barrett in 1910 at Lac Court Oreilles Reservation, Wisconsin.
Denver Art Museum BOj-19

162
Soft Sole Moccasins
Huron, Quebec, mid-19th century.
Moosehair embroidery and cloth trim on dyed leather, 9¼ in.
Until the mid-19th century, clothing dyed with native black walnut husks was popular throughout the northeast. Later, the taste for dark garments persisted in the use of dark trade cloth. Another example of Soft Sole I pattern (see #158).
Denver Art Museum FHr-14

163
Soft Sole Moccasins
Cree, Central Canada, 1870's.
Silk ribbon appliqué on leather, 9¾ in.
Another example of Soft Sole I pattern (see #158).
Denver Art Museum ACe-1

164
Soft Sole Moccasins
Ojibwa, Western Great Lakes, 1969.
Beaded cloth and beaver fur trim on leather, 16 in.
An example of the high moccasins worn today over heavy stockings for snowshoeing. Made at Rat Portage Reserve, Ontario. Another example of Soft Sole I pattern (see #158).
Private Collection

165
Soft Sole Moccasins
Iroquois, New York, early 19th century.
Quillwork and beaded cloth on leather, 8¾ in.
The quillwork includes examples of both plaiting and sewing methods. The beadwork designs have been adapted from earlier moosehair embroidery. An example of Soft Sole II pattern (see #166).
Denver Art Museum VIro-1

•166
Soft Sole Moccasins
Potawatomi, Wisconsin and Kansas, early 20th century.
Leather moccasins with ribbon appliqué cuffs on canvas, 9 in.
Made according to the Soft Sole II pattern, i.e., a gathered toe with no instep section added. See accompanying pattern. The wide cuffs were formerly typical of most midwestern tribes.
Denver Art Museum RPw-3

167
Soft Sole Moccasins
Delaware, Oklahoma, late 19th century.
Beadwork and silk appliqué on leather, 9¼ in.
Another example of Soft Sole II pattern (see #166).
Denver Art Museum BD-22

168
Soft Sole Moccasins
Shawnee, Oklahoma, early 20th century.
Beadwork and cloth trim on leather, 5 in.
Contrast the narrow ankle flaps of these moccasins with the very wide flaps of #166. An example of Soft Sole II pattern.
Denver Art Museum BSh-2

169
Soft Sole Moccasins
Northeastern United States, mid-19th century.
Beadwork on leather, 10 in.
The small ankle flaps of the northeast contrast to the wide flaps of midwestern moccasins. An example of Soft Sole II pattern (see #166). Possibly Delaware.
Denver Art Museum BIro-28

170
Soft Sole Moccasins
Kickapoo, Oklahoma, 1940's.
Beadwork on leather, 10¼ in.
The beaded designs of the ankle flaps came originally from the woven bags produced by the Kickapoo and their neighbors. Later, these designs were adapted for use in both beadwork and ribbon appliqué. An example of Soft Sole II pattern (see #166).
Denver Art Museum: Gift of F. H. Douglas BKp-6

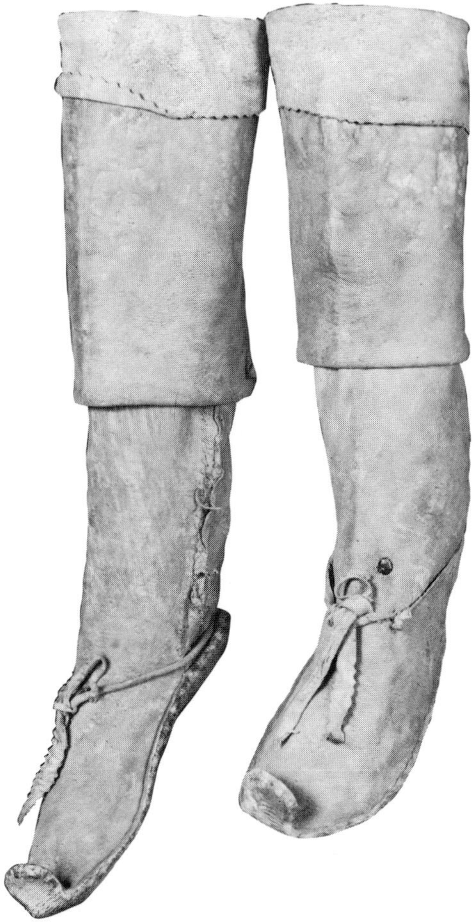

206

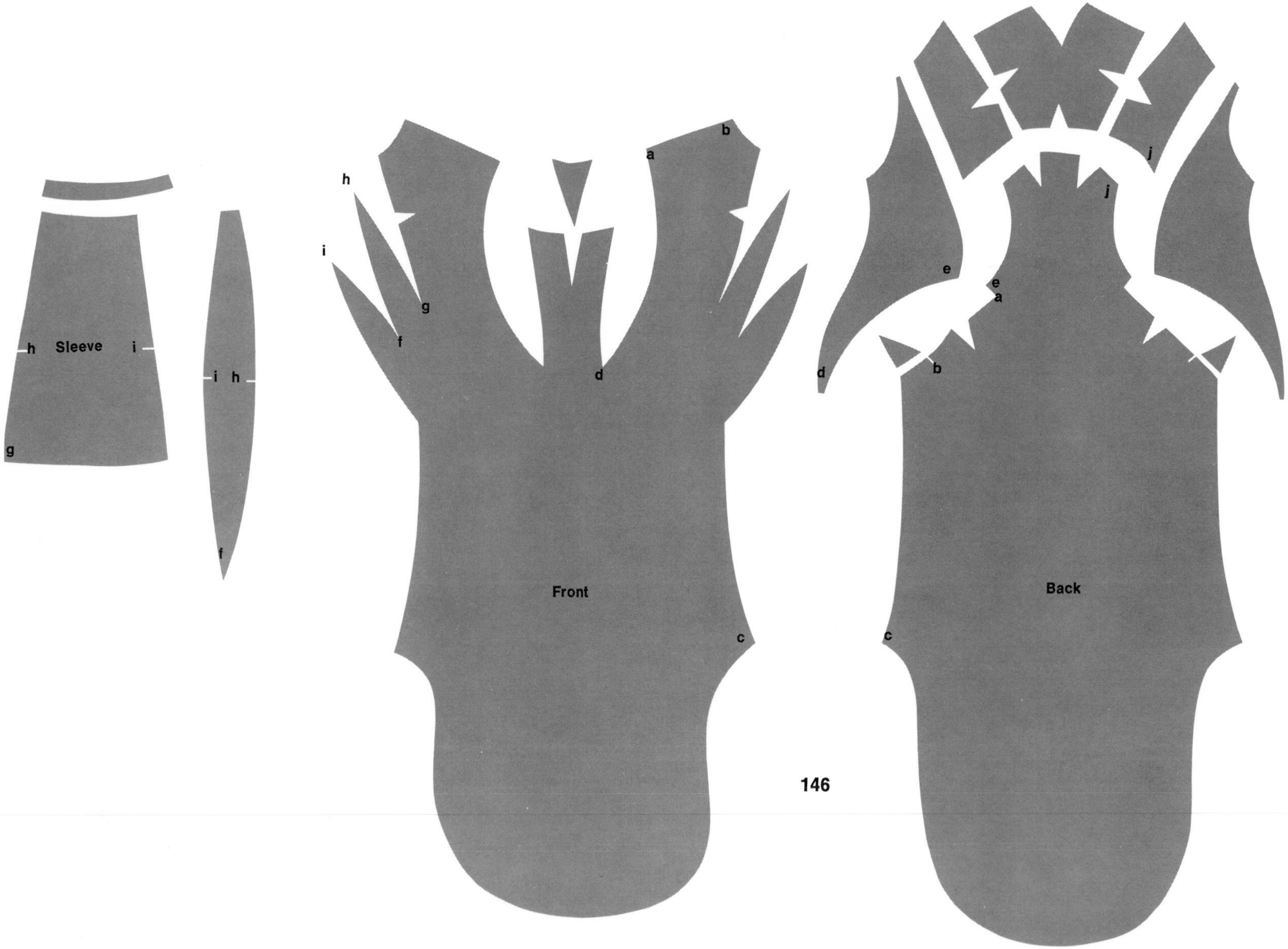

146

146, 154, 155 Designed for warmth, this example of fitted clothing is made of spotted, immature Caribou. Eskimo, Alaska.

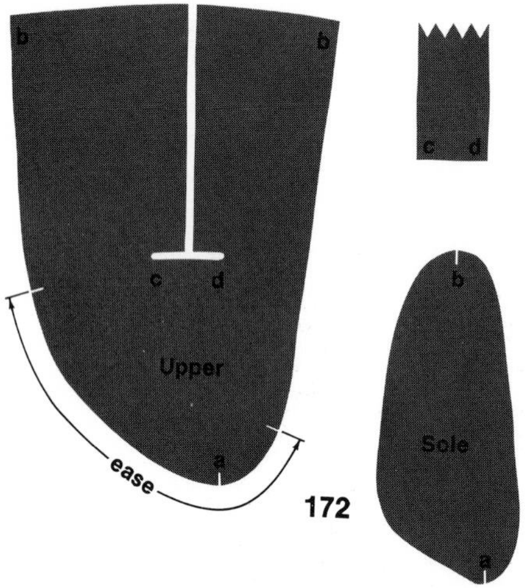

172

171
Soft Sole Moccasins
Seminole, Florida, 1966.
Leather, 11 in.
The maker, Morgan Smith of Big Cypress Reservation, commented that his people often used poor leather for moccasins since they were always wet and soon wore out. An example of Soft Sole II pattern (see #166).
Denver Art Museum LSe-1

•172
Hard Sole Moccasins
Sioux, Dakotas, late 19th century.
Rawhide and quilled leather, 11 in.
The rectangular panel of decoration is an old form, having been recorded in the 1830's. This is the Hard Sole I pattern most common on the Great Plains. See the accompanying pattern.
Denver Art Museum VS-1

•173
Hard Sole Moccasins
Sioux, Dakotas, late 19th century.
Beadwork on leather with quilled trim, 9¾ in.
It has been customary to refer to moccasins with fully beaded soles as "burial moccasins." More likely they were made as gifts for honored friends or relatives. This pair combines geometric designs with natural forms (thunderbirds on insteps and dragonflies on soles) in beadwork. An example of Hard Sole I pattern (see #172).
Denver Art Museum BS-133

174
Hard Sole Moccasins
Cheyenne, Montana and Oklahoma, 1890's.
Rawhide and beaded leather, 10 in.
A good example of the outstanding technical and esthetic qualities of Cheyenne beadwork. Made according to Hard Sole I form (see #172).
Denver Art Museum: Gift of Mrs. E. Q. Smith BChy-120

175
Hard Sole Moccasins
Cheyenne, Montana and Oklahoma, 1890's.
Rawhide and beaded leather, 8 in.
It has been suggested that the U-shaped element in the beadwork derived from earlier Cheyenne moccasins made in Soft Sole I form (see #158). This pair is actually cut in Hard Sole I pattern (see #172) for a girl's use.
Denver Art Museum BChy-138

176
Hard Sole Moccasins
Cheyenne, Montana and Oklahoma, 1890's.
Rawhide and beaded leather, 10¼ in.
The stepped triangles, developed in the 1880's and 1890's, are unique to Cheyenne decorative design. The stylized thunderbirds indicate the moccasins may have been intended for ceremonial use. Made in Hard Sole I pattern (see #172).
Denver Art Museum BChy-47

177
Hard Sole Moccasins
Cheyenne, Montana and Oklahoma, 1890's.
Rawhide and beaded leather, 10 in.
The stylized horses indicate these were made for a man. An example of Hard Sole I form (see #172).
Denver Art Museum BChy-77

178
Hard Sole Moccasins
Arapaho, Wyoming and Oklahoma, late 19th century.
Rawhide with beaded and quilled leather, cloth trim, 11 in.
The four colors of the quillwork symbolize the four cardinal directions. Quilled lines with tufts of yarn or trade cloth were often applied to buffalo robes and tipi linings, but seldom to moccasins. An example of Hard Sole I pattern (see #172).
Denver Art Museum: Gift of Frank Kemp VAr-15

179
Hard Sole Moccasins
Arapaho, Wyoming and Oklahoma, 1860's.
Rawhide and beaded leather, 10⅛ in.
Arapaho beadwork designs are thought to have symbolic meaning in some cases, and this is probably true of these moccasins. Made in Hard Sole I form (see #172).
Denver Art Museum BAr-58

180
Hard Sole Moccasins
Assiniboine, Montana and Alberta, 1942.
Rawhide and beaded leather, 6½ in.
The instep decoration is believed to have been derived from earlier soft sole moccasins (see #158) presumably worn on the northern plains before the introduction of the Hard Sole I pattern by which this pair was made (see #172).
Denver Art Museum BAs-4

172

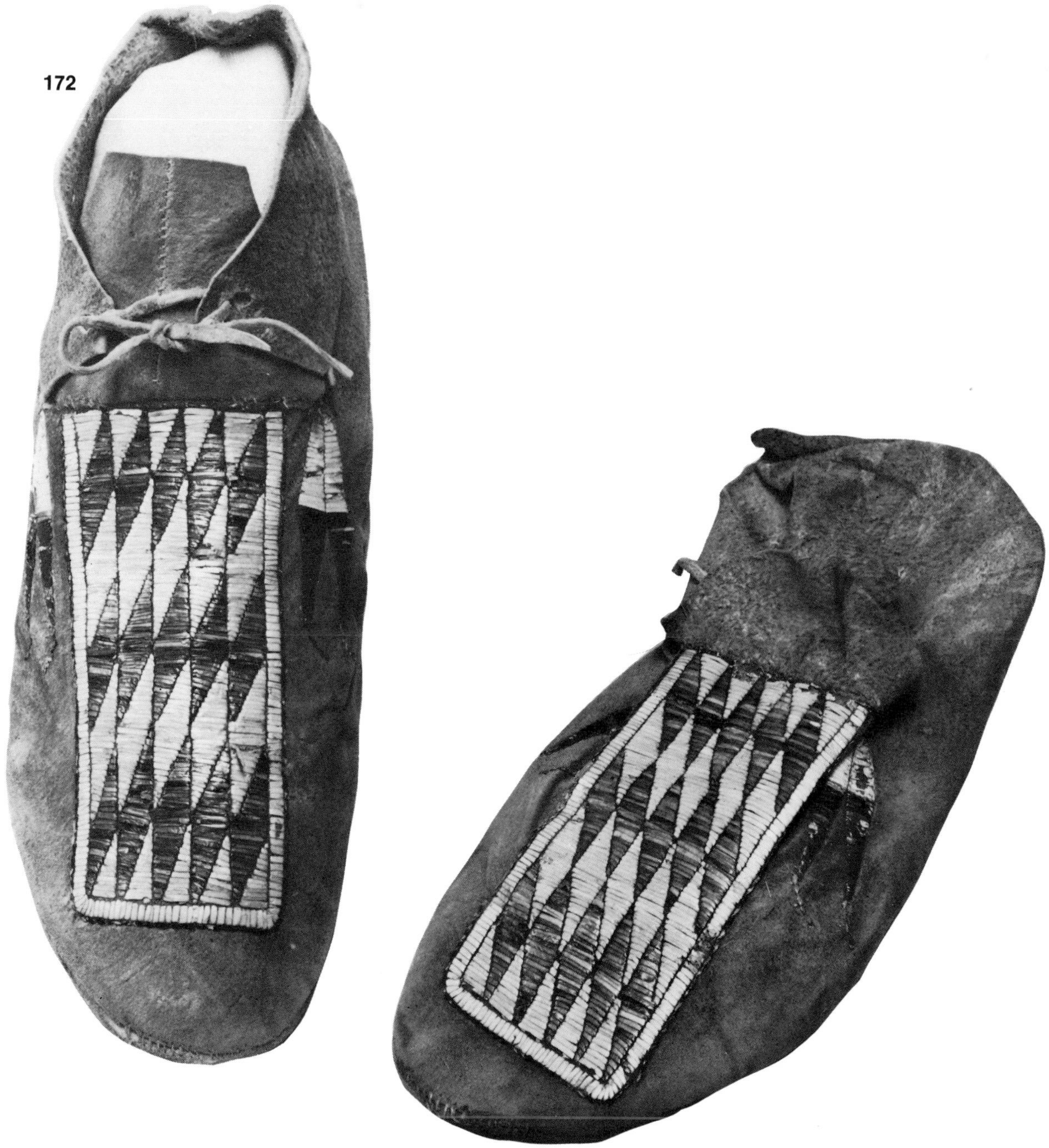

196

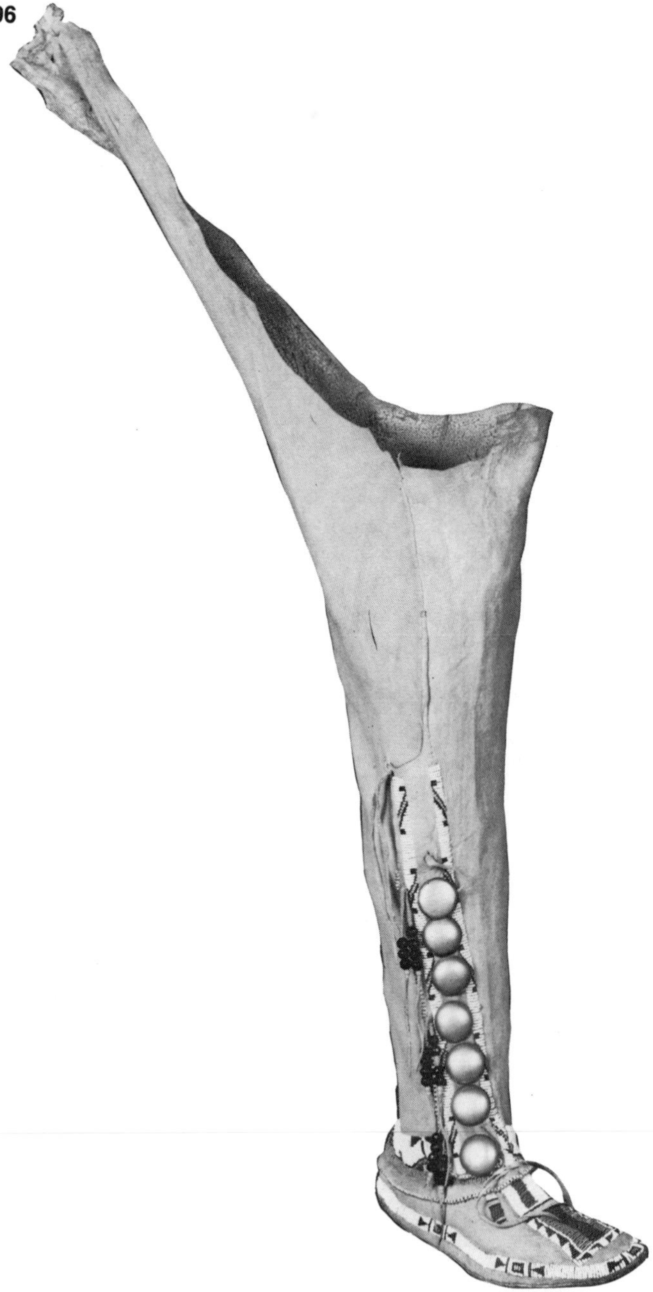

181
Hard Sole Moccasins
Comanche, Texas and Oklahoma, late 19th century.
Rawhide soles, painted and beaded leather uppers, 9½ in.
The long fringes, the paint, and the sparing beadwork are typical of the southern Plains. Unlike most moccasins cut in Hard Sole I form, these also have ankle flaps and small, added tongues.
Denver Art Museum BCm-21

182
Hard Sole Moccasins
Blackfeet (?), Alberta and Montana, 1890's.
Rawhide soles, beaded canvas uppers, 10 in.
An example of the heavily beaded dance moccasins of the late 19th century. This pair may have been made by the neighboring Assiniboine and traded to the Blackfeet. The yellow figures on the tongues represent horse tracks, indicating that the wearer had successfully captured horses from an enemy tribe.
Denver Art Museum: Gift of Thomas Dines, Quigg Newton, Sr., and John Burnett BBI-80

183
Hard Sole Moccasins
Blackfeet (?), Alberta and Montana, late 19th century.
Rawhide and beaded leather, 9¾ in.
See notes for #182. These are women's moccasins, topped with a wrapped ankle flap. Another example of Hard Sole I pattern (see #172).
Denver Art Museum BBI-69

184
Hard Sole Moccasins
Blackfeet, Alberta and Montana, late 19th century.
Rawhide and beaded leather, 10 in.
The light beading is thought to be more typical of Blackfeet moccasin decoration than the fully beaded uppers of the two preceding pieces. The simple floral design represents the western expression of the "double curve" motif. Made in Hard Sole I pattern (see #172).
Denver Art Museum BBI-66

185
Hard Sole Moccasins
Crow, Montana, late 19th century.
Quilled leather, 11¾ in.
An unfinished pair of moccasins, showing the rough shape of the upper. The banded design is often seen in Crow moccasin decoration.
Denver Art Museum VCr-3

186
Hard Sole Moccasins
Crow, Montana, early 20th century.
Rawhide and beaded leather, 10¾ in.
The "keyhole" design was established in the northern plains in the 1830's and persists today. An example of Hard Sole I pattern (see #172).
Denver Art Museum BCr-27

187
Hard Sole Moccasins
Crow, Montana, early 20th century.
Rawhide and beaded leather, 8¼ in.
Another example of the Crow banded moccasin decoration. Hard Sole I pattern (see #172).
Denver Art Museum BCr-101

188
Hard Sole Moccasins
Pawnee, Nebraska and Oklahoma, 1870's.
Rawhide and beaded leather, metal ornaments, 10½ in.
As is often the case, these soles were cut from a painted parfleche. Hard Sole I pattern (see #172).
Denver Art Museum BPn-4

189
Hard Sole Moccasins
Osage, Missouri and Oklahoma, 20th century.
Rawhide and beaded leather, 9¾ in.
The ankle flaps indicate these are women's moccasins. The Osage, like other Plains people, are thought to have once made moccasins in the soft sole style. Very likely the ankle flaps persisted after the adoption of this hard sole pattern.
Denver Art Museum BOs-15

193

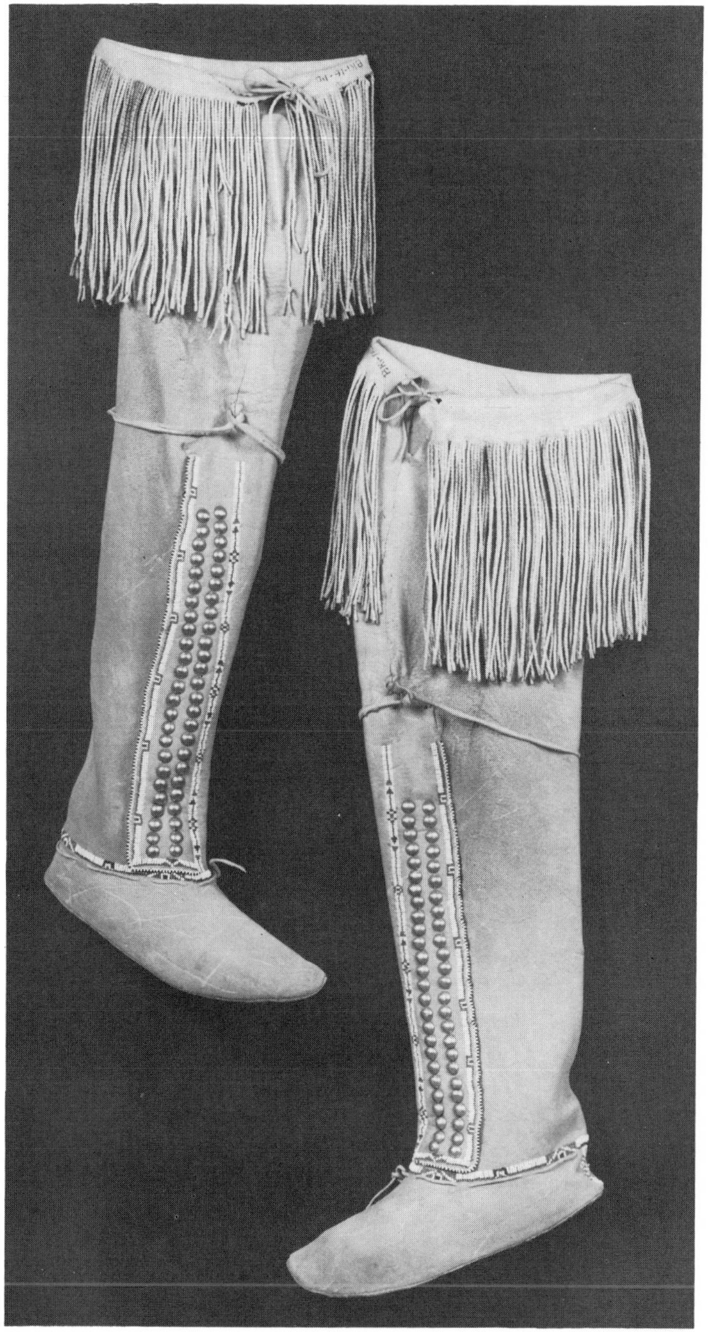

197

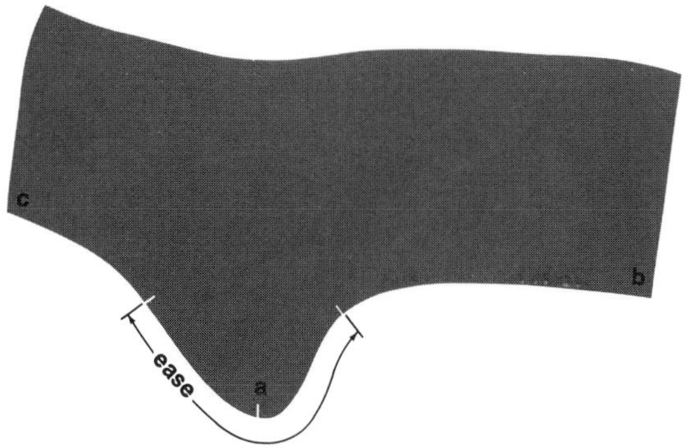

197

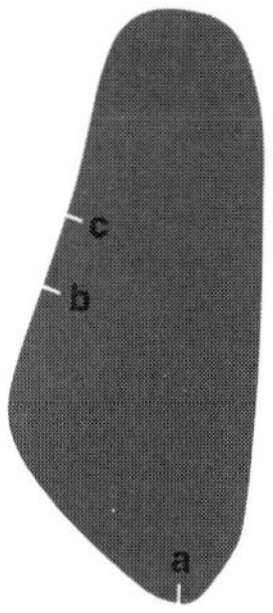

190
Hard Sole Moccasins
Kiowa, Oklahoma, mid-19th century.
Rawhide sole, painted and beaded leather upper, 10¼ in.
An example of early southern Plains moccasin decoration in which beadwork plays a role subordinate to painted leather. Hard Sole I pattern (see #172).
Denver Art Museum BKi-51

191
Hard Sole Moccasins
Kiowa, Oklahoma, mid-19th century.
Rawhide sole, painted and beaded leather upper, 10⅛ in.
Another example of early southern Plains moccasin decoration. Hard Sole I pattern (see #172).
Denver Art Museum BKi-29

192
Hard Sole Moccasins
Kiowa, Oklahoma, mid-19th century.
Rawhide sole, leather upper beaded and trimmed with cloth, 9⅝ in.
An unusual form, unique to the Kiowa, with an exposed seam allowance. In the late 1870's, the Kiowa began constructing moccasins with seam allowances inside as other Plains tribes did.
Denver Art Museum BKi-57

•193
Hard Sole Boots
Kiowa, Oklahoma, late 19th century.
Rawhide sole, painted and beaded leather uppers, metal ornaments, 32½ in.
These moccasin-legging combinations were worn by southern Plains women. This pair shows the sparse beading and fine designs characteristic of old Kiowa art, the German silver ornaments favored by the southern Plains people, and the twisted two-ply leather fringes developed in this region.
Denver Art Museum BKi-16

194
Hard Sole Boots
Kiowa, Oklahoma, early 20th century.
Rawhide soles, beaded and painted leather uppers with metal ornaments, 18½ in.
See note for #193.
Denver Art Museum BKi-3

195
Hard Sole Boots
Arapaho, Wyoming and Oklahoma, 1880's.
Rawhide soles, beaded and painted leather uppers, 20 in.
The Cheyenne and Arapaho women wore hard sole boots similar to those of the Comanche and Kiowa but decorated them more heavily. See #193 for pattern.
Denver Art Museum BAr-29

•196
Hard Sole Boots
Cheyenne, Montana and Oklahoma, late 19th century.
Rawhide soles, beaded and painted leather uppers, metal ornaments, 36 in.
Boots with moderate decoration might be worn with simple trade cloth or leather dresses. See #193 for pattern.
Denver Art Museum BChy-62

•197
Hard Sole Moccasins
Navajo, Arizona, 20th century.
Rawhide soles, dyed leather uppers, silver buttons, 10¾ in.
This Hard Sole II pattern is the basic man's moccasin of the Navajo and Pueblos. The accompanying diagram shows its cut.
Denver Art Museum LN-4

198
Hard Sole Moccasins
Navajo, Arizona, 20th century.
Rawhide soles, dyed leather instep, leather uppers, 9¼ in.
A variant of Hard Sole II pattern, this is the Navajo woman's old-style moccasin with a high wrapped upper. The sewing method has caused the sole to take on a three-dimensional form.
Denver Art Museum LN-13

199
Hard Sole Boots
San Juan Pueblo (?), New Mexico, 20th century.
Painted rawhide soles, leather uppers, 15 in.
The curved sole form of Hard Sole II pattern with simple boot tops. This form is worn still by women at San Juan and other Tewa Pueblos.
Denver Art Museum: Gift of C. W. Douglas LT-2

207 opposite

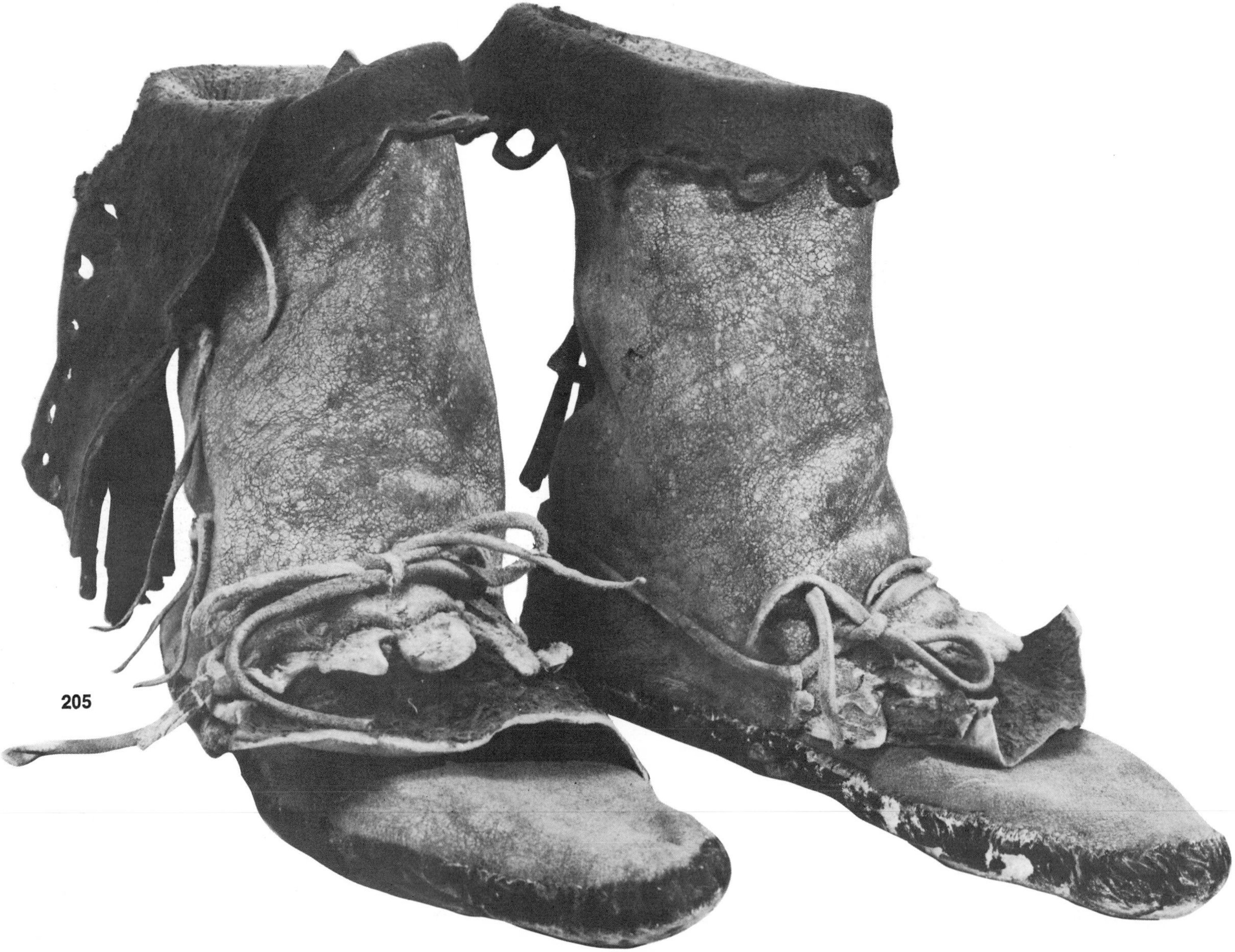

205

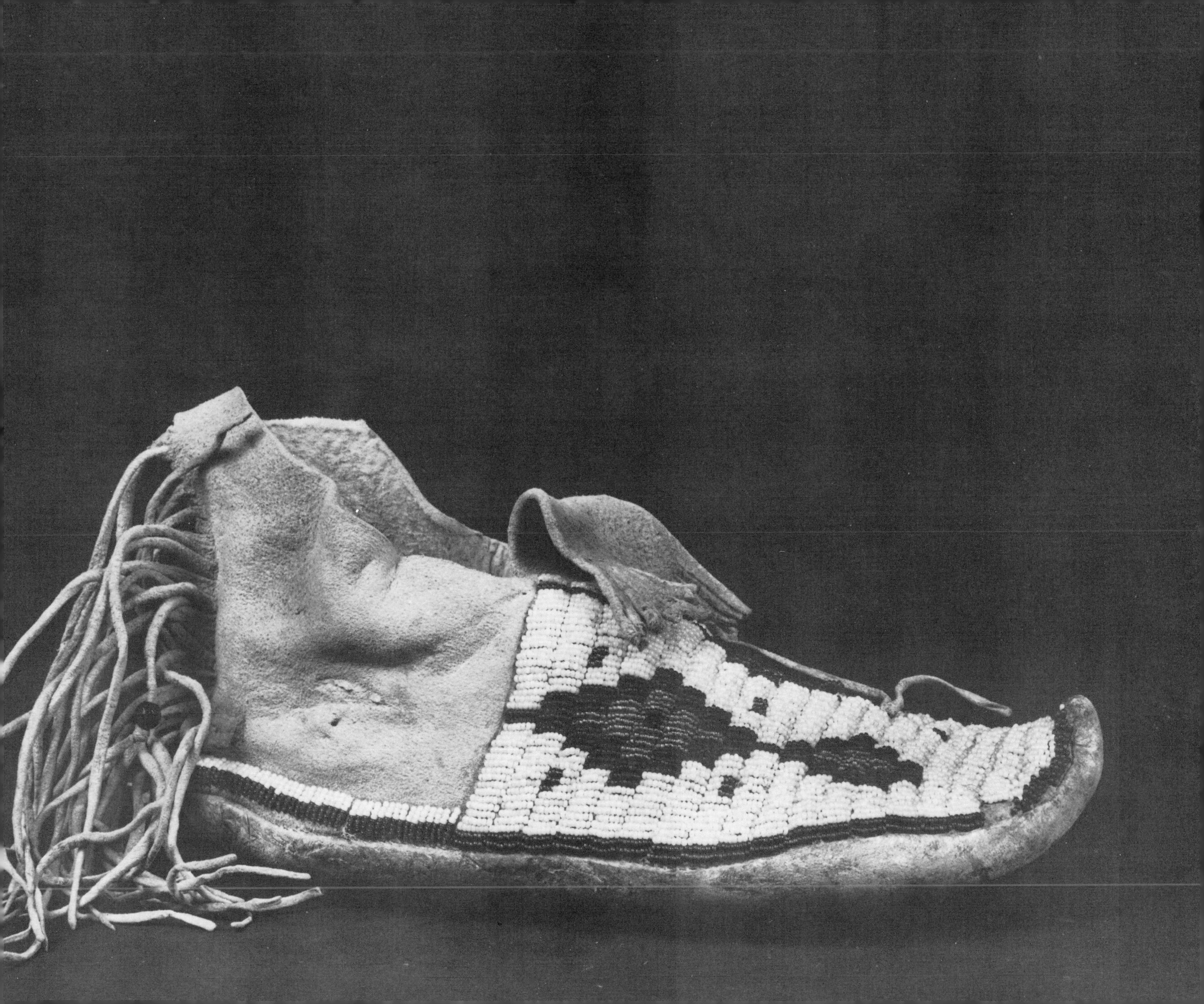

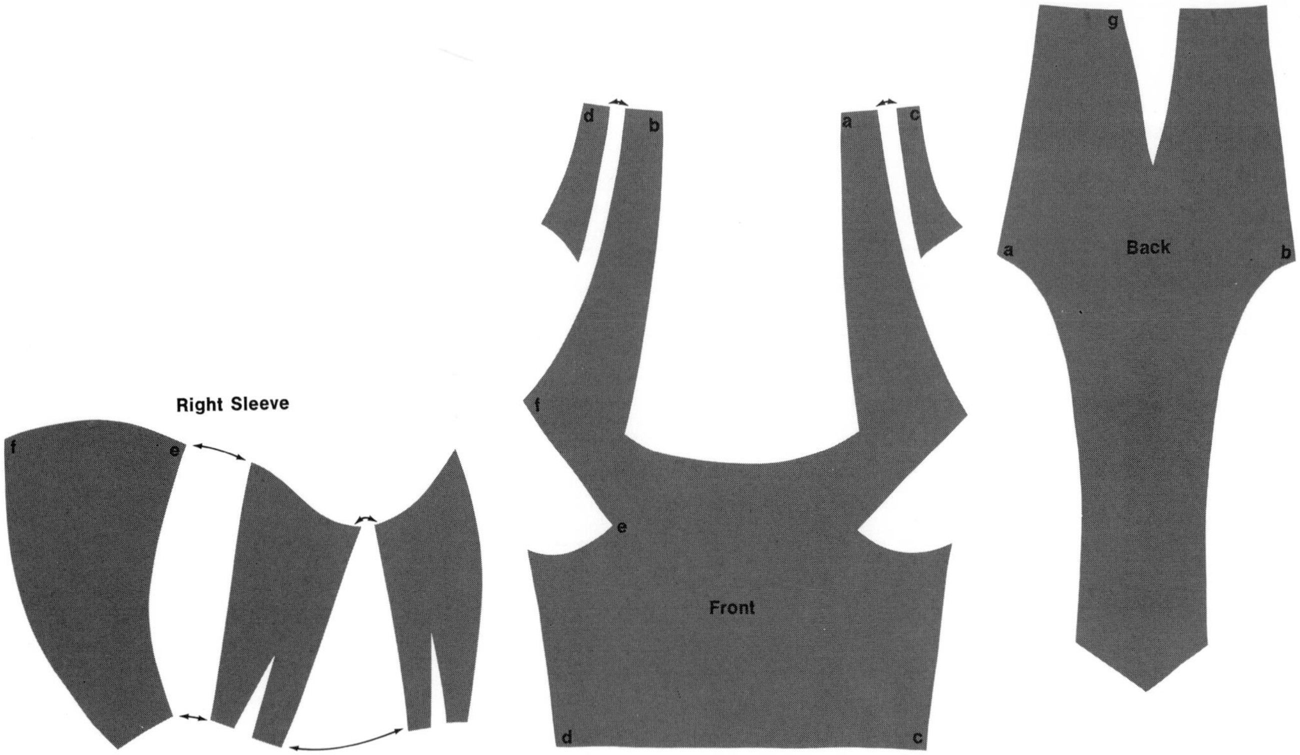

150

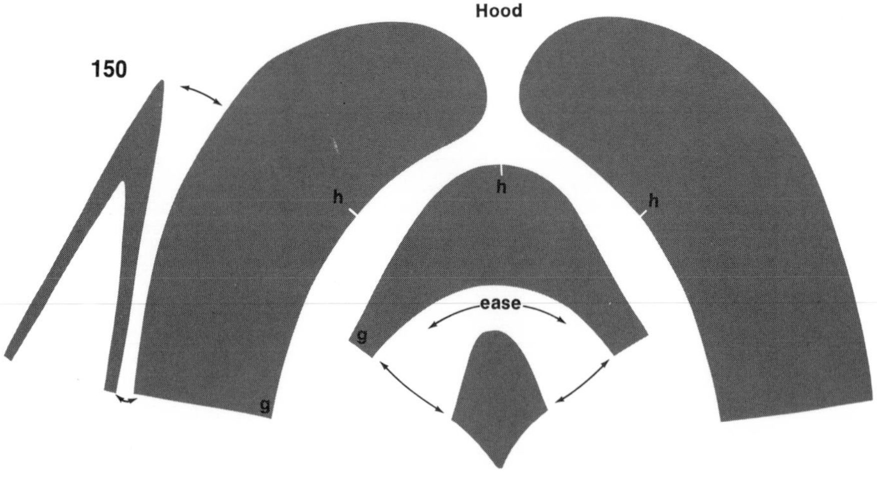

200
Hard Sole Moccasins
Santo Domingo Pueblo, New Mexico, 1967.
Painted rawhide soles, leather uppers, 10½ in.
Men's dancing moccasins with the curved-edge soles of Hard Sole II (see #197).
Denver Art Museum: Gift of Norman Feder LSD-1

201
Hard Sole Boots
Santa Clara Pueblo, New Mexico, late 19th century.
Painted rawhide soles, beaded leather uppers, 15 in.
An unusual variation of Pueblo women's boots. Several other pairs of beaded boots from Santa Clara Pueblo exist in various museum collections, but little is known of the origin of this decoration.
Denver Art Museum BSC-1

202
Hard Sole Moccasins
Acoma Pueblo, New Mexico, 20th century.
Painted rawhide soles, leather uppers, 8¼ in.
Another variation of the Hard Sole II form worn by Pueblo women. The moccasin upper is wrapped around the leg and then the long leather strips are wound over this, much like puttees.
Denver Art Museum LAc-1

203
Hard Sole Boots
Taos Pueblo, New Mexico, 20th century.
Rawhide soles, leather uppers, 15 in.
The woman's boot with deep folds is unique to Taos. It may have been inspired by Spanish boot forms or by the closer-fitting Apache folded boots (see #206).
Denver Art Museum: Gift of the heirs of Allen Tupper True LTa-11

204
Hard Sole Moccasins
Pueblo, New Mexico, 20th century.
Rawhide soles, leather uppers with silver buttons, 10 in.
Similar to #202. The moccasins are worn with separate leather wrappings.
Denver Art Museum: Gift of Oraivi Gallery LPb-6

•205
Hard Sole Boots
Zuni Pueblo, New Mexico, late 19th century.
Painted rawhide soles and leather uppers, 7½ in.
Polychrome leather boots are still worn by masked dancers at Zuni and in the several Hopi villages. The instep is further decorated with leather cutwork.
Denver Art Museum PZu-12

•206
Hard Sole Boots
Chiricahua Apache, Arizona, late 19th century.
Rawhide soles, painted leather uppers, 33 in.
Apache shoe forms have the curved soles of Navajo and Pueblo shoes, as well as the unique toe forms shown here. These men's boots were worn in deep folds or fully extended as necessary. Hard Sole pattern III.
Denver Art Museum LAC-2

•207
Hard Sole Moccasins
Jicarilla Apache, New Mexico, late 19th century.
Rawhide soles, beaded leather uppers, 10⅝ in.
The Jicarilla favored pointed toes in contrast to the larger toe projections of the western Apache (#206). Hard Sole III form.
Denver Art Museum: Gift of F. H. Douglas BAJ-27

208
Hard Sole Moccasins
Jicarilla Apache, New Mexico, late 19th century.
Rawhide soles, beaded and painted leather uppers, 11¼ in.
Cut in the Jicarilla variant of Hard Sole III form with the pointed toe, but decorated like moccasins of the adjacent southern Plains tribes. For a man.
Denver Art Museum BAJ-25

209
Hard Sole Moccasins
Mescalero Apache, New Mexico, late 19th century.
Rawhide soles, beaded leather uppers, 10 in.
Another example of Hard Sole III form.
Denver Art Museum BAM-6

147

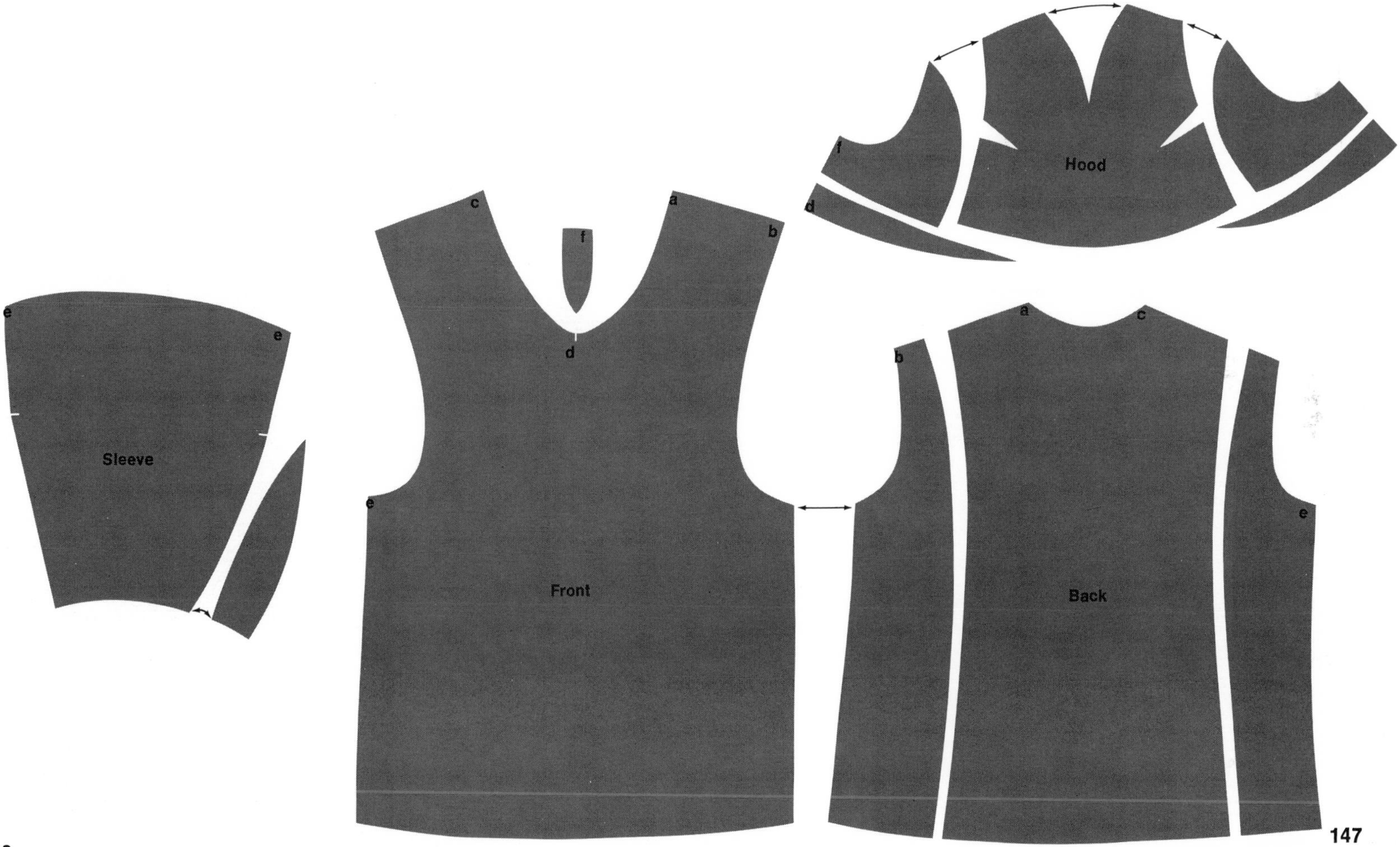
Hood
f
d
c
a
b
f
d
Front
e
Sleeve
e
e
a
c
b
Back
e

The Crowning Touch

The Crowning Touch

Perhaps no other aspect of his costume offered the Native American such a rich field for the free play of his imaginative impulses as his hairstyle and headdress. The cliché of the Indian with a feather headdress is, like most stereotypes, accurate enough — as far as it goes. Feathers indeed played a role in hair and head decoration, but they were only one element in an extensive repertoire. So many and varied were the styles of hair and headdress worn for practical, ceremonial, magical, social, and solely decorative purposes that we can do no more than suggest their astounding diversity.

Over much of North America people simply parted their hair along the center, brushed it well, and allowed it to hang free. This treatment showed off the hair to some advantage, but often suggested further elaboration, such as painting the part red (cat. #1) or even daubing the hair itself with paint — usually in horizontal streaks at eye level. Mojave men along the lower Colorado River rolled their hair into 20 to 30 sausage-shaped coils which were "fixed" with mesquite gum or mud and sometimes decorated with white clay paint. Throughout most of the 19th century, men of the northern Plains arranged the hair on the back of their heads into a dozen or more bunches and then "set" these at regular intervals with pitch. When dry, the pitch was painted white and a few ornaments added. By the late 19th century, the northern Plains dandies must have tired of washing the pitch from their hair because they began making separate switches or hairpieces that could be tied on.

Native Americans usually took great pride in their long, fine hair and seldom cut or trimmed it except as a sign of mourning. Although clipped hairstyles popular in other parts of the world generally found little favor in North America, the so-called "Mohawk" or roached haircut was worn by warriors of most native groups in the eastern United States and

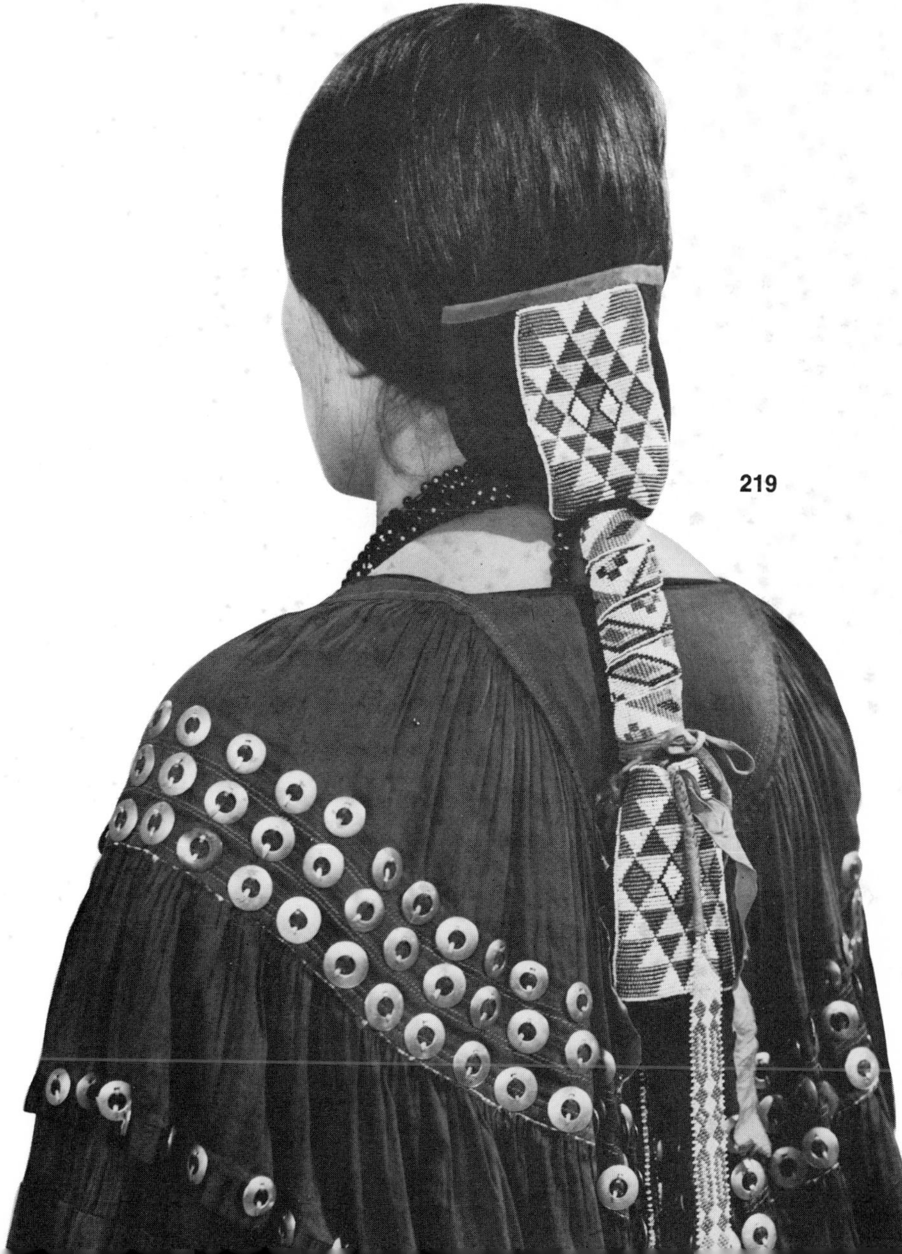

219

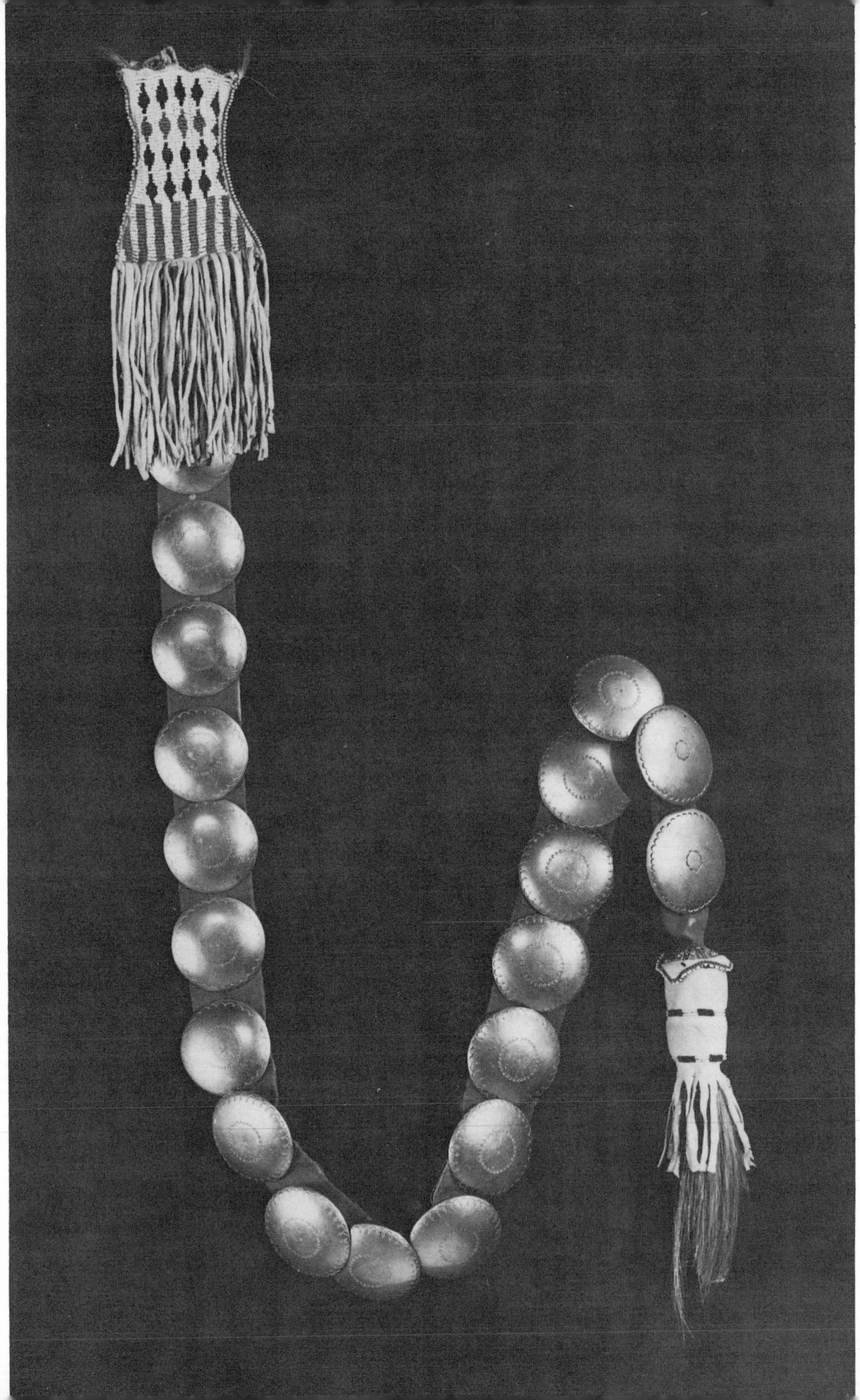

221

224

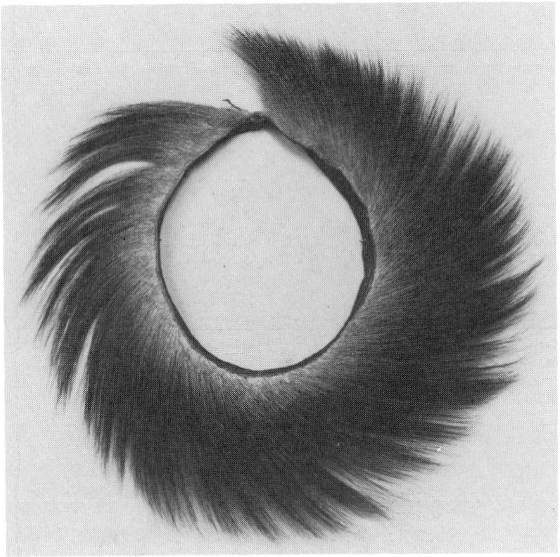

228

as far west as the central Missouri River valley. This style was created by cutting off all but a central ridge of hair with one long lock just behind the crown left intact — the scalp lock. Tightly braided and decorated with a feather or ornament, the scalp lock served as a badge of valor, a symbol of the fighting man's fatalistic outlook: "See how unafraid I am to die in battle! Here's my scalp — try to get it!" Frequently, this short-cut hair served as a base for a spectacular headdress of porcupine and deer hair, also called a roach (cat. #267).

Braids were worn by many tribal groups who also favored loose hair styles. Further, some hairdresses combined both sorts of hair styles — braids at the sides with loose hair down the back, for example. On the northern plains especially, changing local fashion frequently dictated new combinations of loose and braided locks. Nonetheless, some hairdresses achieved lasting and widespread popularity. Most common of all were the braids worn by women over much of North America and by men throughout most of the west. In the northeast and midwest, women often braided their hair into one plait at the nape. Blackfeet men and their neighbors to the north and west wore three braids — two at the sides and one in back. Crow and Shoshone men went one step further by combing out a separate forelock to stand erect when painted with pitch or clay.

Sleekly braided hair provided the perfect foil for colorful decoration. Materials used for wrapping braids — strips of otter or beaver fur in the western United States, bright felt strips at Taos and some adjacent pueblos — complemented the hair in both color and texture. Women on the plains and in parts of the intermontane region added braid ties, small beaded rectangles tied into collars at the top of the braid. In the east and midwest, the single braid style gave rise to two handsome types of hair ornaments, the hair binder and hair bow. The first was a piece of beaded material wrapped around the folded back braid and tied in place with a long strip of beadwork (cat. #219). A distinctive ornament with long pendants, the hair bow was simply tied around the back braid. Prehistoric eastern women wore similar hair bows of polished stone (which archaeologists find today) and perhaps of perishable materials as well. Recent hair bows are made of trade materials — cloth, ribbons, and metal ornaments. When German silver first became available to men of the southern and central Plains, they created their own version of the hair bow: the round disk, or concha, to be tied into a back hairlock. In time, multiple conchas were set into bands or "hair plates" (cat. #221), which must have been as heavy and uncomfortable as the pitched hair style had been inconvenient, for they had almost gone out of fashion by the 1870's. Women of the central arctic still wear "hair sticks," polished wooden rods to which the braids are secured by strips of beaded cloth that mask the hair completely.

The "shongo" of the southwest, in which the hair is combed into one or two smooth masses bound at the nape or over the ears, illustrates another basic type of Native American hairstyle. Allan Houser's charming painting *Herding Sheep* shows a Navajo mother and her children wearing such single shongos (cat. #224). The Pueblo peoples once used special hand-woven haircords to arrange their shongos while the Navajo more often fastened theirs with hand-spun native wool yarn. Unmarried Hopi girls have created an unusual shongo by parting the hair in the center and winding each side tightly over a special wooden form. After tying, the "roller" is removed and the hair spread gently into circular whorls. Because this light and graceful style is abandoned for the more practical braids of the housewife when the Hopi girl marries, the name "butterfly," given to it by Europeans, seems particularly apt.

229

248 Appropriately named the "Bighead," the ceremonial headdress pictured here was worn at the harvest festival by a member of the Maru cult. Pomo, California.

The attention lavished on hairdress and hair ornaments is also reflected in an incredible variety of Native American hats and headdresses. Some head coverings were designed for utilitarian purposes alone — for protecting the wearer against excessive cold or heat, glaring sun, or rain. Eskimo parkas have built-in hoods for protection against fierce cold, but elsewhere in North America separate caps and hoods of fur or leather were worn. Head coverings to guard against both heat and glare were commonplace in regions of strong sun like the plateau, where sunshades were made from the long mane of the moose (cat. #228), and the plains, where painted rawhide visors were used for this purpose (cat. #229). In the arctic, Eskimo hunters made wooden or ivory goggles to minimize the blinding glare of sun on snow. Although the Aleutian Islands see little sunshine, Aleut men devised special wooden hats to reduce the glare of sun on water as they hunted in skin boats. These hats were made of thin boards, steamed and bent into a conical form. Less substantial, but just as effective, were the leaf wreaths made by the farmers of Taos and other pueblos. Basketry rain hats, woven tightly enough to resist water and sometimes waterproofed further with a coat of native paint (cat. #234), served double duty when painted with heraldic figures to announce family and clan affiliations.

Native Americans are truly unsurpassed as designers of ceremonial headdresses. Cortez and his officers had never seen anything like Moctezuma's magnificent headdresses of quetzal feathers. They were in fact so impressed that they "borrowed" one to send their king. It is still on view in a museum in Vienna. In this country and in Canada, many early Europeans commented upon the startling, overwhelming headdresses worn by natives in council meetings, at tribal ceremonies, and even into battle. These ceremonial head coverings exist in so many varieties that we can only briefly indicate something of the range of their designs, materials, and functions.

In the Puget Sound region of Washington state, where native religions centered on personal supernatural guardians who initiated their human associates into the possession of magical power and

247

260

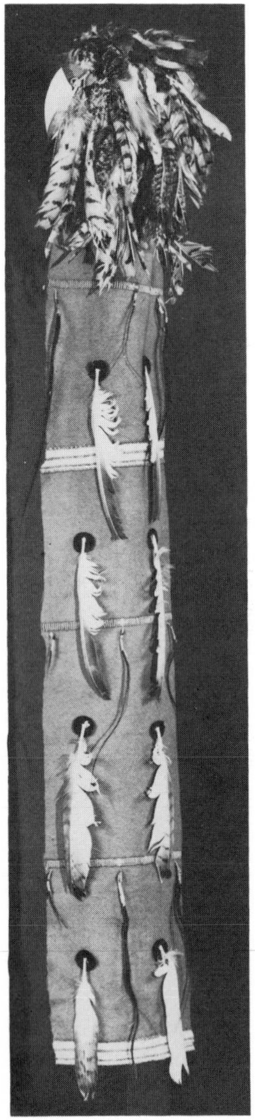

taught them dances to be performed at the winter solstice, the most potent and feared spirits were *Tobchadad,* the warriors. Those who had received the power of these spirits wore, during their vigorous dance, a conical headdress of human hair and eagle feathers called a "sharphead" (cat. #247). In action, the hair locks and feathers are agitated violently, contributing to the inspiring force of the dance.

Today, many Americans have heard of the Ghost Dance movement of the 1890's through accounts of the massacre of Wounded Knee suffered by Sioux participants in this religious revival. The underlying idea of the Ghost Dance — a return to native ways and a rejection of all things foreign — also spread to tribes in California and led in time to the establishment of the Maru cult. One of the dances of this society was the "Bighead," whose striking headdress (cat. #248) may have originated in a dream or may represent, as one author has suggested, a field of flowers in bloom. Since the dance itself is a kind of harvest festival, the headdress more likely refers to edible wild plants.

In the northwest corner of California, native people considered it their heaven-ordained duty to gather and preserve "wealth objects" such as obsidian, bright feathers, and certain marine shells, which were made into clothing or ceremonial properties and exhibited to the Supreme Being at an annual "World Renewal Ceremony." By this act they proved how faithfully they had obeyed their god's directions and expressed their hopes that he would allow the world to exist for yet another year. Many of these wealth objects show exquisite workmanship because the more perfect their execution the more efficacious they were thought to be in gaining the favor of the deity (cat. #250).

Although not strictly ceremonial, some of the special clothing associated with Plains warfare was intended magically to insure safety and success in battle. Each warrior sought alliance with a supernatural "familiar" who gave him the means to protect himself, often including instructions for special headdresses or garments that would confer invulnerability. Roman Nose, the famous Cheyenne leader, for example, arrayed himself in a spirit-inspired warbonnet supposed to render him bulletproof. Made in response to its owner's religious vision, each of these protective headdresses was thus a sacred object in its own right (cat. #258).

However, the best-known Plains Indian head decorations were the feathers a warrior tied into his hair to designate his battlefield exploits. Karl Bodmer's portrait of the Arikara warrior Pachtuwa-chta shows this sort of decoration (cat. #266). Here the feathers notched and marked with red indicate that he was wounded while attacking enemies in battle. Other feathers, worn in specified positions or marked in certain ways, spoke an elaborate symbolic language of valorous deeds.

Another class of Plains head coverings indirectly associated with warfare were actually insignia for military or quasi-military societies. Each tribe had several men's societies that were oriented directly toward war — like the Cheyenne Dog Soldiers or the Kiowa Kaitsenko — or toward some related end such as maintaining internal order in tribal camps. Membership in these groups was based partially upon proven fighting ability, and society members frequently took part in military expeditions together. Each society had special regalia purportedly "dreamed" by the founder and worn at society functions and sometimes even into battle (cat. #260).

Similar insignia was worn by civil leaders — tribal and band chiefs — across the continent. In the case of the feathered caps worn by Huron village chiefs (cat. #271), it is the embroidered headband rising to a single peak in front that proclaims its wearer a "first man" or leader of his village. In the southeast, chiefs wore turban-like hats of cloth wrapped over a fiber foundation and decorated with silver headbands and plumes of native egret or imported

250

272

ostrich to indicate their rank. The noted Creek chief McIntosh sat for his portrait in the 1830's wearing such a headdress (cat. #272). Along the northwest coast, there were no chiefs in the strict sense, but rather leaders of clans and family lineages who stood preeminent in their villages and who often distinguished themselves by wearing the finest clothing available. Although no specific garments were reserved to village leaders alone, dances in which only such persons and their families might join often occasioned special costuming. One of these was the Sisaok dance of the Bella Coola, which required an unusual headdress surmounted with a wooden plaque carved to represent the dancer's crest (cat. #270). Precious materials — ermine pelts, abalone shell inlays — emphasize his wealth.

Like people all over the world, Native Americans sometimes made and wore hats merely for decorative effect. Two good examples of such hats — both made in twined basketry and worn only by women — come from the western United States. On the plateau fez-like hats covered with false embroidery in native fibers or trade wool yarn added a jaunty touch to the costume and proclaimed the skill of the weaver, who was presumably also the wearer (cat. #243). The native women of California, among the world's foremost basket makers, made little caps of excellent technical and esthetic quality. Like the Plateau hat, these caps were usually covered with false embroidery in various natural fibers and served no practical, religious, or socially significant purpose (cat. #238).

A complete collection of the hundreds of headdress forms made in Native America would fill several museum galleries. Our few examples can only hint at the variety of their functions and designs, but even this small sampling proves the Native Americans second to none in inventiveness and imagination.

258

Hairdresses and Headdresses

210
Dusty Dress, Kalispel
Edward S. Curtis, American, 1868-1952.
Sepia photograph, 22 x 18 in.
The girl's hair has been painted with stripes of white clay.
From *The North American Indian* by Edward S. Curtis (Norwood, Mass., 1911), Supplemental Folio VII, pl. 238.

211
Mojave Hairdress
Lower Colorado River area, mid-19th century.
Replica, Denver Art Museum Workshop.
The coils of hair were originally fixed into place with mesquite gum or mud and painted with white clay.
After *Handbook of the Indians of California* by A. L. Kroeber, Bulletin 78 of the Bureau of American Ethnology (Washington, D.C., 1925), p. 729.

212
Pitched Hair Ornament
Crow, Montana, 1880's.
Pitched and painted human hair, beaded tie band, 36 in.
This piece was worn around the back of the head and tied over the forehead.
Denver Art Museum FCr-21

213
Massika and Wakusasse, Sauk and Fox Indians
Karl Bodmer, Swiss, 1809-1893.
Hand-colored lithograph, 23 x 17 in.
Both men wear animal hair roaches over their own roached hair. A portion of Massika's scalp lock is visible.
Denver Art Museum: Bequest of F. H. Douglas IP-141

214
Missouri Indian, Oto Indian, Chief of the Puncas
Karl Bodmer, Swiss, 1809-1893.
Hand-colored lithograph, 21½ x 16½ in.
The two men left and center have roached haircuts with scalp locks.
Denver Art Museum: Bequest of F. H. Douglas IP-129

215
Mexkemahuastan, Chief of the Gros Ventres of the Prairies
Karl Bodmer, Swiss, 1809-1893.
Hand-colored lithograph, 20¼ x 15½ in.
The coiled topknot indicates that the man is owner of a medicine pipe.
Denver Art Museum: Bequest of F. H. Douglas IP-131

216
A Medicine Pipe, Piegan
Edward S. Curtis, American, 1868-1952.
Sepia photograph, 22 x 18 in.
Showing both the medicine pipe (see #215) and the late 19th century Blackfeet man's hairdress with the part to one side.
From *The North American Indian* by Edward S. Curtis (Norwood, Mass., 1911), Supplemental Folio VI, pl. 199.

217
Swallow Bird, Apsaroke
Edward S. Curtis, American, 1868-1952.
Sepia photograph, 22 x 18 in.
This striking hairdress was worn principally by members of the Crow (or Apsaroke) Lumpwood Society. In this case, the finished coiffure has been painted with clay.
From *The North American Indian* by Edward S. Curtis (Norwood, Mass., 1909), Supplemental Folio IV, pl. 134.

218
Braid Wrappings
Kiowa, Oklahoma, mid-19th century.
Otter fur with beadwork, 43 in.
In use, the fur was wound around the braids. From the family of Satank (Sitting Bear), a noted Kiowa man.
Denver Art Museum FKi-3

•219
Hair Binder
Sauk and Fox, Oklahoma and Iowa, 1880's.
Binder of beaded cloth, wrapping of woven and braided beadwork, 49 in.
This ornament is possibly related to the hairbow (see #220) which is known to have existed since prehistoric times. Both were worn by women only.
Denver Art Museum BSF-4, 31

220
Hair Bow
Delaware, Oklahoma, late 19th century.
Felt panel with ribbons and metal ornaments, 44¼ in.
A recent version of an ornament with an ancient history.
Denver Art Museum JD-7

•pictured in catalog

•221
Hair Plates
Cheyenne, Oklahoma, 1870's.
German silver disks on cloth with beaded leather ornament, 62 in.
A man's ornament, worn tied to the back hair.
Denver Art Museum JChy-27

222
Hair Plates
Kiowa, Oklahoma, mid-19th century.
Shell disks on cloth, 9 ft.
Very long hairplates were worn by men on horseback.
From the family of Satank (Sitting Bear), a noted Kiowa man.
Denver Art Museum FKi-2

223
Hair Sticks
Caribou Eskimo, Keewatin Territory, Canada, 20th century.
Beaded cloth bindings, wooden sticks, 12 in.
Another ornament inspired by contact with adjacent Indian groups. Worn only by women.
Private Collection

•224
Herding Sheep
Allan Houser, American, b. 1915.
Tempera on paper, 28¼ x 18¼ in.
The artist, himself an Apache, shows the shongo hairdress worn by Navajo and Pueblo people.
Denver Art Museum: Santa Fe Railroad Presentation Award PAC-3

225
Hair Cord
Pueblo, New Mexico, 20th century.
Native cloth of cotton and wool, 43 in.
Used to tie a shongo hairdress.
Denver Art Museum: Gift of the Estate of F. H. Douglas RPb-40

266

271

226
Loitering at the Spring
Edward S. Curtis, American, 1868-1952.
Sepia photograph, 22 x 18 in.
A group of Hopi girls, showing the "butterfly" hairdress of unmarried women.
From *The North American Indian* by Edward S. Curtis (Norwood, Mass., 1922), Supplemental Folio XII, pl. 400.

227
Cap
Jicarilla Apache, New Mexico, 19th century.
Beaver fur and trade cloth, 8 in. dia.
An example of the simple caps worn throughout most of North America for warmth.
Denver Art Museum FAJ-1

•228
Eye Shade
Nez Percé, Idaho, 1870's.
Moose mane, 16 in. dia.
A strip of skin from the moose's hump is tanned and used as the basis of this hat. Worn by both sexes.
Denver Art Museum FNP-1

•229
Sunshade
Arapaho, Wyoming and Oklahoma, mid-19th century.
Painted rawhide, 14¼ in.
Denver Art Museum PAr-5

230
Snow Goggles
Eskimo, Alaska, 20th century.
Ivory, 5¼ in.
Worn to minimize the glare of sun on snow and ice.
Denver Art Museum QEsk-112

231
Snow Goggles
Eskimo, Pt. Hope, Alaska, late 19th century.
Wood with sinew cord, 4¾ in.
Wood is more commonly used than ivory for snow goggles since it is less apt to freeze to the wearer's face.
Denver Art Museum QEsk-565

232
Hunting Hat
Eskimo or Aleut, Western Alaska, 1880's.
Bent and painted wood, ivory trim, 12 in.
Such hats were often worn by men hunting from kayaks and served in part to minimize the glare of sun on water.
Collected by Father Mercier, a Catholic missionary, on the Kuskokwin River.
National Museum of Man of Canada, Division of Ethnology IV-E-90

233
Basket Hat
Tlingit, Alaska, late 19th century.
Twined basketry in spruce root, painted with native pigments, 16 in. rim dia., 7½ in. high.
This is the basic basket hat style of the northern Northwest Coast. The painting depicts a raven, the wearer's crest.
Denver Art Museum YTl-146

•234
Basket Hat
Tlingit, Alaska, late 19th century.
Twined basketry in spruce root, painted with native copper oxide, 17¼ in. rim dia., 7 in. high.
The native blue paint serves both as additional waterproofing and as a "wealth" color. The Tlingit used natural copper as a sculpture material and as the basis for paint and dye.
Denver Art Museum YTl-148

235
Basket Hat
Gulf of Alaska region, early 19th century.
Twined basketry in spruce root, painted with native pigments and trimmed with glass beads, 12 in. rim dia., 5½ in. high.
An unusual early form made by the northern Tlingit and their Eskimo neighbors along the Gulf of Alaska.
Denver Art Museum YTl-149

•236
Basket Hat
Nootka, Vancouver Island, British Columbia, late 19th century.
Twined basketry in cedar bark, native pigments, 12¼ in. rim dia., 5¾ in. high.
The bowl-form hat was standard among the Nootka and the coastal Salish groups to the south.
Denver Art Museum YHi-23

237
Basket Hat
Nootka, Vancouver Island, British Columbia, early 20th century.
Twined basketry in cedar bark, 12 in. rim dia., 6¾ in. high.
An everyday hat, worn primarily as protection against rain.
Denver Art Museum YNu-28

•238
Basket Hat
Hupa, Northwestern California, 20th century.
Twined basketry in various natural materials, 6¼ in. rim dia., 3½ in. high.
The customary woman's cap of northwestern California.
Denver Art Museum YHu-25

239
Basket Hat
Karok, Northwestern California, 20th century.
Twined basketry in various natural materials, 7 in. rim dia., 3½ in. high.
As exemplified here and in #241, Karok basketry caps are not always completely covered with false embroidery. They differ in this respect from those made by neighboring peoples.
Denver Art Museum YKa-25

240
Basket Hat
Karok, Northwestern California, 1880's.
Twined basketry in various natural materials, 7 in. rim dia., 3 in. high.
An older example than the others included here, this hat shows that the basic concept of the woman's basket cap has changed little in the past 100 years.
Denver Art Museum YKa-56

241
Basket Hat
Karok, Northwestern California, 20th century.
Twined basketry in various natural materials, 6¼ in. rim dia., 3 in. high.
The soft red is seen more often in Karok basketry than in that of neighboring groups.
Denver Art Museum YKa-44

242
Basket Hat
Karok, Northwestern California, late 19th century.
Twined basketry in various natural materials,
6¾ in. rim dia., 4 in high.
Denver Art Museum YKa-63

•**243**
Basket Hat
Nez Percé, Idaho, early 20th century.
Twined basketry in natural materials,
7 in. rim dia., 6 in. high.
The typical Plateau woman's hat. This example is covered with false embroidery in natural fibers, but later examples are decorated with trade yarn.
Denver Art Museum YNP-40

244
Woman's Hat
Nez Percé, Idaho, 20th century.
Beadwork on canvas, cloth lined,
7 in. rim dia., 6¾ in. high.
Plateau basketry hats like #243 are seldom made today. They have been replaced with copies like this, made of cloth and fully beaded.
Denver Art Museum BNP-1

245
Shaman's Crown
Tsimshian (?), British Columbia, late 19th century.
Bear claws, bird quills, etc., on leather base, 9 in. outside dia.
Worn by shamans (native doctors) in curing the sick.
Denver Art Museum FTI-4

246
Head Ring
Kwakiutl, Vancouver Island, British Columbia, mid-19th century.
Cedar bark with calico lining, 9 x 6¼ x 3½ in.
All participants in the Kwakiutl Winter Dances wore head rings of some type except when masked. The precise form of the rectangular front and back plates differs according to the dancer's role.
Collected by George T. Emmons.
Denver Art Museum YKw-3

•**247**
Sharphead
Coast Salish, British Columbia and Washington, late 19th century.
Human hair locks on cloth and rawhide base, 38 in.
The headdress associated with dances by individuals possessed by Tobchadad, the warrior spirit (see text).
Denver Art Museum FKw-2

•**248**
Bighead
Pomo, California, late 19th century.
Tule rushes, wooden rods, various feathers,
4 ft. outer dia.
The Bighead dancer appeared at a harvest festival of the Maru cult, a society whose mission was to induce a return to old ways and to reject all European influences.
Lowie Museum of Anthropology, University of California, Berkeley, 1-79474, 1-79487, 1-79480, 1-79492, 1-79485, 1-79476, 1-79509, 1-2803, 1-211591

249
Hair Net
Yurok, Northwestern California, late 19th century.
Painted netting of wild iris fiber, feather trim, 32 in.
Worn over hair tied at the nape by Yurok men at the World Renewal ceremonies.
Denver Art Museum RYu-1

•**250**
Ceremonial Headband
Pomo, Central California, late 19th century.
Woven base of native fiber, feathers of woodpecker and California quail, ornaments of abalone and clam shell, 22 in.
One of the many headdress forms worn in dances of wealth display and World Renewal (see text).
Denver Art Museum RPo-4

251
Shaman's Crown
Karok, Northwestern California, 19th century.
Padded leather base, decorated with woodpecker scalps and other materials, 11 in. outer dia.
Worn by a female shaman in curing. The feathers and other decorative materials are wealth objects supposed to increase the effectiveness of the doctor's efforts.
Denver Art Museum: Gift of Mrs. Donald Bromfield FKa-5

238

243

252
Hairpin
Pomo, Central California, late 19th century.
Engraved crane wing bone bound with various feathers (oriole, bluebird, woodpecker, and California quail), added ornaments of flicker quills, clam shell disks, and abalone pendants, approx. 13 in. Pomo men and women bound their hair in a knot at the nape and tucked one or more of these decorated pins into it. The various ornaments are wealth objects considered proper for ceremonial wear.
Denver Art Museum FPo-7, 8

253
Hairpin
The mate to #252.

254
Hairpin
Pomo, Central California, late 19th century.
Wood base bound with flicker feathers and bird's down, 26½ in.
A variant of the more common hairpin form (see #253), but also worn on ceremonial occasions.
Denver Art Museum FPo-14

255
Ceremonial Headdress
Blackfeet, Alberta and Montana, late 19th century.
Quilled and painted rawhide base, quilled and painted leather "reliquary" on forehead, various ornaments including ermine tubes and eagle feathers, approx. 28 in.
The central figure of the Blackfeet Sun Dance is the Holy Woman, who wears this headdress during specified parts of the ceremony.
This example belonged to Coming Singing.
Denver Art Museum FBI-27

256
War Headdress
Blood, Alberta, mid-19th century.
Beaded leather and brass base with ornaments of ermine tubes and quilled eagle feathers, 16 in.
A protective war charm made for Weasel Moccasin, a Blood man. The brass disk symbolized the sun, the ultimate source of power.
Denver Art Museum FBI-46

257
Medicine Crow, Apsaroke
Edward S. Curtis, American, 1868-1952.
Sepia photograph, 22 x 18 in.
The hawk fastened to the subject's head shows how protective war headdresses were worn. Medicine Crow had received instructions for making and wearing this amulet in a vision.
From *The North American Indian* by Edward S. Curtis (Norwood, Mass., 1909), Supplemental Folio IV, pl. 117.

•258
War Headdress
Winnebago, Wisconsin and Nebraska, mid-19th century.
Buffalo horns and grizzly bear claws on rawhide base, various ornaments, 20 in.
Another example of an individual's vision-inspired protective headdress.
Denver Art Museum FWin-6

259
War Headdress
Blood, Alberta, mid-19th century.
Fur cap with tuft of feathers, all painted with native ochre, approx. 8 in. dia., 6 in. high.
Many Mules was a noted "collector" of enemy horses and scalps. This cap was part of his protective medicine. Most war headdresses are actually ornaments tied into the hair (see #256). This one is unusual because it is more substantial.
Denver Art Museum FBI-33

•260
Military Society Headdress
Blackfeet, Alberta and Montana, mid-19th century.
Cap of various feathers on felt base, pendant of beaded strouding with various ornaments, 65 in. overall.
A headdress worn by officers of the Dog Society, whose original function was to guard camps against surprise attack and who had specified duties in the Sun Dance ceremony.
Denver Art Museum FBI-14

261
Military Society Headdress
Sioux, Dakotas, 1880's.
Decorated eagle feathers on leather base, beaded browband, 67 in. overall.
The Sioux formerly had a group of men's societies called the Akichita (soldiers). Officers of these groups, who also functioned as leaders in battle, wore so-called "war bonnets" of eagle feathers as symbols of their rank. Today, such headdresses have become the insignia on the "elite" — distinguished older men — who wear them on fesitve occasions.
Denver Art Museum FS-16

262
War Honors Headdress
Sioux, Dakotas, late 19th century.
Quilled rawhide base with ornaments of feathers and horse tail, 26½ in.
The wapageniki was an ornament tied to a man's back hair. It held the eagle feathers that were marked to indicate his war exploits.
Denver Art Museum VS-16

263
Woman's Society Headdress
Blackfeet, Alberta and Montana, 1870's.
Buffalo skin with horns, feathers, and beaded browband, 39 in. overall.
The Mahtoki were a society of Blackfeet women whose function was to attract buffalo herds within range of the hunters. They did this by wearing buffalo skin headdresses and dancing in imitation of these animals. The society still exists today although its function has changed.
Denver Art Museum FBI-8

264
Always Howling Woman
Winold Reiss, American, 1888-1953.
Oil on canvas, 48 x 36 in.
The subject, an officer of the Mahtoki Society, wears the group's distinctive headdress (see #263) with a buffalo robe and a variant of the deer tail dress.
The Anschutz Collection

236

265
Mato-Tope, Chief of the Mandans
Karl Bodmer, Swiss, 1809-1893.
Hand-colored lithograph, 23½ x 17 in.
The subject wears several symbols of his brave deeds. On his headdress, for example, is a knife painted red to indicate that he used such a knife to stab an enemy warrior.
Denver Art Museum: Bequest of F. H. Douglas IP-151

•266
Pachtuwa-Chta, Arikara Warrior
Karl Bodmer, Swiss, 1809-1893.
Hand-colored lithograph, 23 x 17 in.
The subject wears several hair feathers, marked and colored in reference to his battlefield exploits. Also note the beaded blanket strip which decorates his buffalo robe.
Denver Art Museum: Bequest of F. H. Douglas EI-203

•267
Roach
Sioux, Dakotas, early 20th century.
Porcupine guard hair, dyed deer hair, 16 in.
The roach of animal hair probably began in the east as an adjunct to the roached haircut. Later, it appeared on the plains as part of the insignia of the Omaha Dance, a quasi-military society. Today it is the preferred headdress for active dancers.
Denver Art Museum FS-28

268
Roach
Sioux, Dakotas, 1958.
Porcupine guard hair, dyed deer hair, 14 in.
An example of the roach worn by young men today for social dances.
Private Collection

269
Roach
Menomini, Wisconsin, late 19th century.
Wild turkey beard, dyed deer hair, base 5 in.
The midwestern people often wore this small variant of the roach as part of their war insignia. Note the unusual material, turkey beard, used in place of the customary porcupine guard hair.
Denver Art Museum FMen-1

•270
Chief's Headdress
Bella Coola, British Columbia, mid-19th century.
Base of native matting and cloth, wooden frontal with abalone shell inlay, ornaments of sea lion bristles, ermine skins, and trade cloth, 43 in. overall.
The Sisaok was a society reserved for those of chiefly status. Members dance in headdresses like this example. The carved figure of the frontal is a hawk, the crest of the wearer. The hollow top was filled with eagle down which scatted about during the dance to indicate the chief's good will and generosity.
Denver Art Museum QBC-3

•271
Chief's Headdress
Huron, Quebec, 1924.
Moosehair embroidery on leather, hawk feathers, 10 in.
The single peak of the headband indicates that the wearer is first chief of his village.
Denver Art Museum FHr-7

•272
McIntosh, a Creek Chief
Unknown lithographer after portrait by Charles B. King, 1837.
Hand-colored lithograph on paper, 20 x 14 in.
The subject wears the Southeastern chief's turban-like hat. This example is decorated with a silver headband and plumes of various birds.
Denver Art Museum: Bequest of F. H. Douglas IP-31

273
Southeastern Man's Costume with Chief's Headdress
Creek-Seminole, Georgia and Florida, mid 19th century.
Headdress only: cloth turban with silver headband and plume of egret feathers, 14 in.
The whole costume is representative of those worn by Southeastern men in the 1830's and 1840's. The turban was the insignia of a village chief.
Denver Art Museum FSe-1, JD-3

Mixed Bag | European Influence

Mixed Bag: European Influence

As European society advanced across the American continent, the native people responded to the impact of alien cultural influences in a variety of original ways. As we have already seen, the availability of European manufactured goods offered a new world of possibilities in clothing decoration. Metal jewelry, glass beads, and cloth were eagerly welcomed and quickly adapted to native traditions of clothing design and decoration. Direct borrowings of European clothing concepts and even literal copies of European fashions soon followed although ingenious hybrid garments combining foreign and native ideas frequently resulted. Whenever a European garment was copied in native leather, for example, pattern adjustments were unavoidable. Leather is more flexible than cloth, but it lacks that "straight of goods" orientation according to which European clothing patterns were cut. Native leather behaves, in fact, as though it were bias cut in every direction. On the other hand, leather responds very well to fringing while cloth does not.

Outside of the arctic and subarctic, trousers were unknown in Native America until introduced by the Europeans. After the movement onto reservations, leather trousers began to be made that followed European prototypes quite closely, even incorporating pockets and front fly openings. Frequently, though, the cut of the seat of the pants was often simplified because the maker could depend upon the elasticity of the leather to provide the proper fit. The same flexibility made it possible to convert leggings into trousers by adding leather pieces to make a seat. In the example included here, the trousers open at the sides and were evidently meant to be worn with suspenders.

When cloth trousers first went on sale at trading posts, they were very expensive, and the native men who bought them took pains to make them last, for they soon noticed that, in spite of its advantages, cloth tore easily and soon became ragged. The Metis of Canada, a people of mixed native and European ancestry, devised half-leggings to wear over cloth trousers to protect them from rough use. Leather rectangles rolled around the lower leg and gartered below the knee, these half-leggings were decorated with paint and embroidery and eventually became acceptable parts of dress clothing (cat. #277), but their practicality soon recommended them to other native people as well as the European employees of fur trading companies.

Shirts and parkas indigenous to Native America had been, without exception, pullovers. Front-opening European shirts and coats were a novelty that quickly inspired square-cut adaptations in both leather and trade cloth. Cut as rectangles with sleeves set in on straight seam lines, these jackets were not fitted garments, but something more like a binary shirt with a vertical front opening. Occasionally, however, native seamstresses made more thoroughgoing copies of European garments like the Cree coat shown here, which is cut exactly like a mid-19th century frock coat (cat. #279). Made in native leather and decorated with fine quillwork, it is a handsome example of the harmonious mixing of the two clothing traditions. Another striking example of the European front-opening coat was the wedding coat of the Osage. According to tradition, an officer of the U.S. Dragoons gave such a coat to an Osage chief, who dressed his daughter in it on her wedding day as proof of his high esteem. Thus, a cloth coat in military style became *de rigueur* for an Osage bride. Commercially made copies of military dress cutaways complete with epaulets, the wedding costume was made even more spectacular with the addition of beadwork, silk appliqué, and other native decorations.

Native America also adopted another European front-opening garment, the vest, actually worn more often than the coat. Ready-made European vests

293, 294 These fine examples of Seminole patchwork technique show European influence in their styling. Seminole, Florida.

were easily adjusted to native taste with the addition of traditional decorative materials. Occasionally, native seamstresses cut a vest in an approximation of the European fitted style (cat. #284), but they usually followed a more simple binary cut, with straight sides and square shoulders (cat. #283).

Another interesting cross between the front-opening European coat and the square-cut native binary shirt was the capote, a man's outer garment with sleeves and a hood. Front-opening and ranging anywhere from hip to mid-calf in length, capotes were most often made of heavy wool trade blankets (cat. #286), but a few were cut of leather (cat. #287). Although it incorporated the distinguishing characteristics of the European overcoat in its front opening and hood, the capote retained the simple rectangular cut of the indigenous binary shirt — probably less as a matter of preference than as a concession to the thickness of the unfamiliar woven material of which it was most often made.

Although several kinds of fur and leather mittens had been part of the native clothing repertoire, the idea of gloves with separate housings for each finger and decorative wrist gauntlets was a European introduction. Beautiful copies of European gloves have been made at one time or another in most of Native America, and even today native craftswomen produce them for sale and home use. Usually cut according to the foreign pattern but beaded or quilled according to local fashion, gloves offer another example of the perfect melding of European construction with native decorative concepts.

The Victorian mores of the middle and late 19th century indirectly influenced Native American costumes. European fashions dictated by excessive concern for keeping the body "under wraps" exerted a lasting influence on native groups whose clothing forms had never been determined by such inhibitions. Even as they adopted these Victorian styles, they did so for reasons far removed from those which motivated their European contemporaries. On the northwest coast, for example, men and women of important families bought the most expensive European clothes they could afford and wore them as status symbols along with their native heraldic accessories. The Tlingit woman of the 1890's might have worn a silk dress, fashionable hat, kid gloves, and heeled shoes. To this ensemble she would add a silver bracelet or two and some cloth ornaments beaded with her family crest designs. Her male counterpart might have decked himself in grey striped trousers, a boiled shirt, and black jacket, as well as the familiar native ornaments.

In the southwest, Pueblo women had worn sleeveless wrapped dresses for centuries. In the 1880's they added calico underdresses to cover the bare skin of shoulder and arms these dresses exposed to the disapproving eyes of genteel foreigners settling in their homeland. Pueblo women today still wear similar underdresses for such secular events as the Santa Fe Fiesta. But for native ceremonials, it's back to the basic black.

When the Navajos were forced into concentration at Fort Sumner, New Mexico, in the 1860's, they came into daily proximity with European women for the first time. Seeing wives of officers and civilian officials promenading about in full skirts and fitted velvet basques evidently provoked the Navajo women to emulation, for they began making their own version of the ensemble soon after their release. This Victorian-inspired combination of velveteen blouse and full velveteen or calico skirt (cat. #291) persists even today to such an extent that the Navajo fashion has created a continuing demand for velveteen that has sustained the industry through two depressions! The Apaches, who managed to maintain a greater degree of freedom than their Navajo cousins, were nonetheless influenced by Victorian dress. The Apache women made full, gathered skirts like the Navajos, but they chose to wear them in combination with loose calico blouses (cat. #292) which were cooler and more comfortable than the Navajo velveteen style.

By the 18th century, Southeastern native men were wearing garments evidently derived from the European tail coat (cat. #272), as well as ready-made European-style muslin shirts or homemade copies. The English or French man's shirt of the time was full, with sleeves gathered at both wrist and shoulder, a basic form that still survives in the Seminole shirts worn today although the plain or figured calico of which they were originally made has given way to a distinctive patchwork first invented in the late 19th century (cat. #293). The popular woman's costume of the late 19th century was a gathered skirt worn with a full-sleeved blouse featuring a large, flounced collar (cat. #294). In recent versions of this dress, the skirt is made of patchwork and the flounced collar has grown so large as to eclipse the blouse.

Even these few examples suggest how practically and imaginatively Native Americans approached the new ideas of clothing design introduced by Europeans: they adjusted these unfamiliar concepts to native materials and explored ways to use new goods to advantage in traditional clothing forms. We have marveled at the inventive skill of the Native American in developing his personal decorative arts, but we have no better proof of his creative genius than in his ability to assimilate and transform new concepts from the encroaching European tradition.

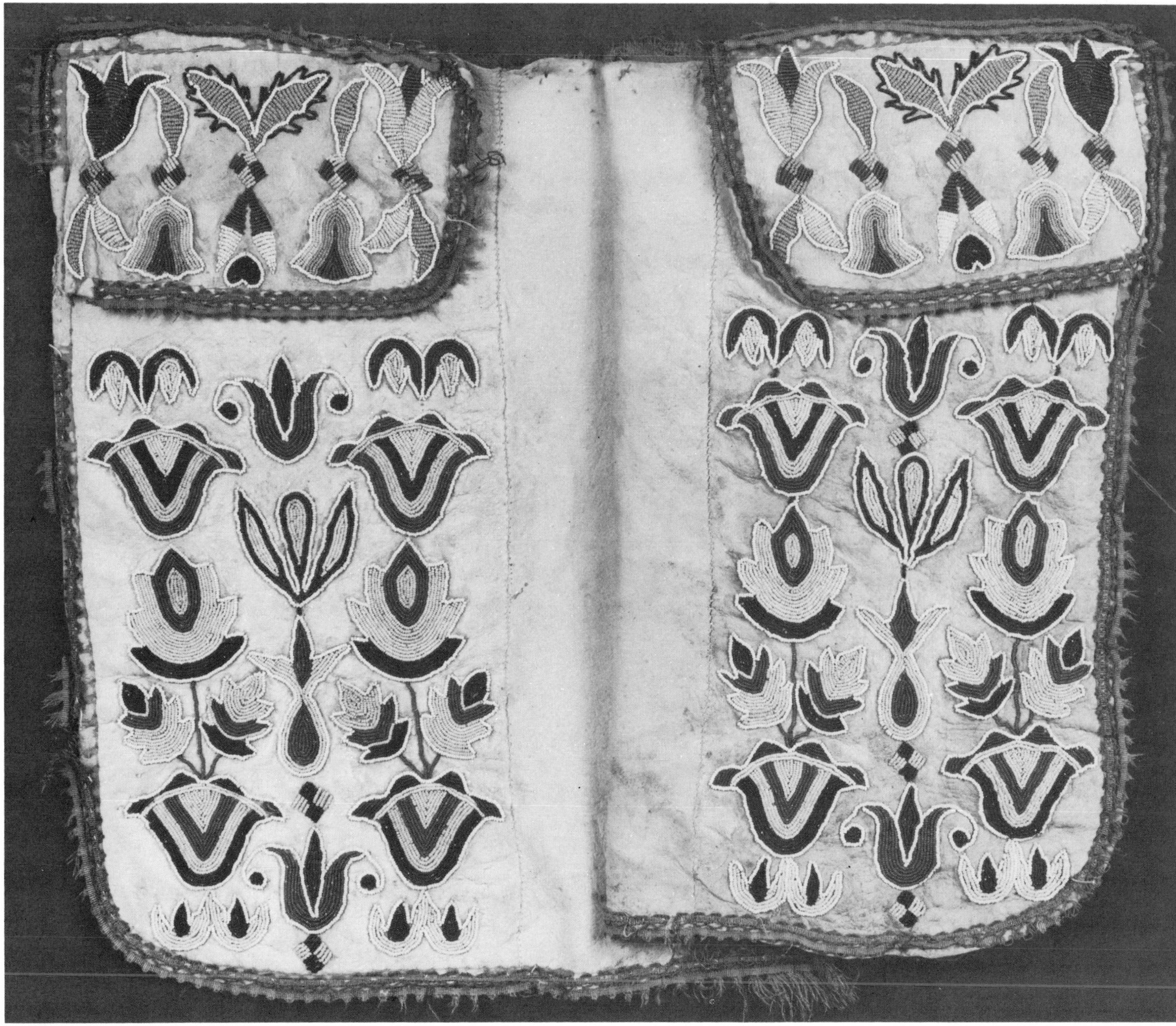

287

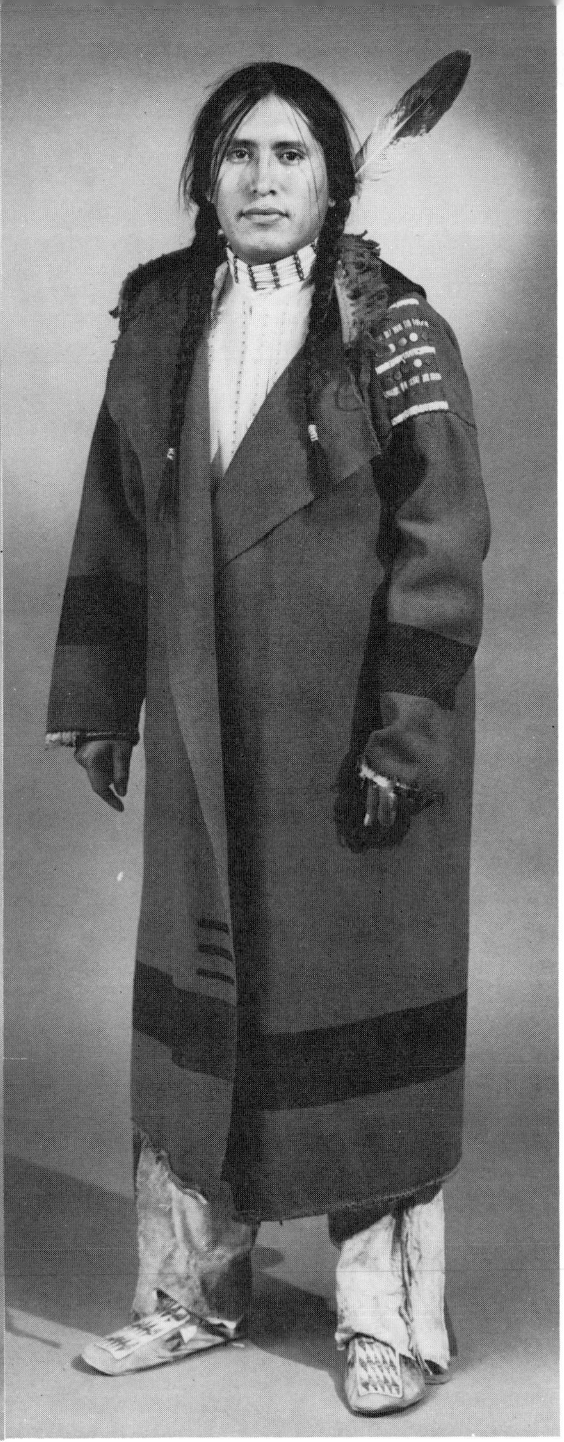

286

Garments Based on European Models

274
Trousers
Crow, Montana, 20th century.
Beaded leather, 40 in.
Simplified European cut reproduced in native leather. The morning glory designs, typical of the 1930's, are rendered in contoured beading.
Private Collection

275
Trousers
Crow, Montana, 20th century.
Beaded leather, 39 in.
A slightly later pair than #274. Roses have replaced morning glories as the stylish flower, and the designs are now worked in a variant contoured beading process.
Private Collection

276
Trousers
Ute, Colorado and Wyoming, late 19th century.
Beadwork on painted leather, 47 in.
A pair of Ute leggings converted to trousers by adding a seat of native leather.
Denver Art Museum BU-95

•277
Half Leggings
Metis, Manitoba and Saskatchewan, mid-19th century.
Beaded leather with cloth lining and trim, 17 in.
The Metis, a people of mixed native and European ancestry who lived on the northeastern plains, invented this garment form as a means of protecting the bottoms of expensive cloth trousers from heavy wear.
Denver Art Museum BRR-1

278
Binary Jacket
Crow, Montana, 20th century.
Beaded leather, 27 in.
The cut resembles that of a contemporary western jacket. The roses that decorate this jacket are worked in a needlepoint beading technique that replaced contoured beading in the 1940's. Compare #274 and #275.
Private Collection

•279
Frock Coat
Metis or Plains Cree, Manitoba and Saskatchewan, mid-19th century.
Quilled leather with cloth trim, 39 in.
This precise copy of a European garment is cut of native materials. Such pieces were made as dress garments for important native men or as gifts for Europeans — fur company officials, visiting dignitaries, and the like.
Denver Art Museum VCe-1

279 - 280

•280
Vest
Matching vest to #279.
Denver Art Museum VCe-2

281
Frock Coat and Vest
Eskimo, Southern Alaska, early 20th century.
Caribou furs, ivory buttons.
Another example of European garments reproduced in native materials. The Eskimo seamstress has finished her work with bands of fur mosaic.
Eastern Washington State Historical Society 531.1, 531.2

282
Frock Coat
Osage, Oklahoma, late 19th century.
Commercial frock coat with epaulets; beading, silk appliqué, and German silver ornaments added; 42 in.
The prototype of this garment was a military coat reportedly presented by an officer of the U.S. Dragoons to an Osage, who loaned it to his daughter for her wedding. This example, like others worn by later Osage brides, came from a commercial costumer. The last Osage wedding in which the bride was bedecked in this kind of costume was celebrated about 30 years ago.
Denver Art Museum AOs-28

•283
Vest
Sioux, Dakotas, 1890's.
Beaded leather with quilled fringe, 19 in.
The vest has been cut with square sides in accordance with earlier native garments. The beadwork designs are typical of the late 19th century. Formerly owned by John White Wolf.
Denver Art Museum: Gift of Mrs. Donald Abbott BS-103

•284
Vest
Santee, Minnesota, c. 1870.
Beaded leather fronts, cambric back from commercial vest, 20 in.
This example is cut like a European vest. The art of the Santee, a people living between the plains and the Great Lakes, reflects influences from both regions.
Denver Art Museum BSt-1

285
Vest
Ojibwa, Western Great Lakes, late 19th century.
Beaded cloth, 20 in.
Another vest cut on the "square" as opposed to fitted European vests. The beading is representative of the Minnesota Ojibwa.
Denver Art Museum: Gift of Miss Anne Evans BS-43

•286
Capote
Northern Plains, 1870's.
Wool blanket with beaded trim, 46 in.
The pattern of this front-opening topcoat is well suited to the particular demands of the heavy trade blanket from which it is made.
Denver Art Museum R-61

•287
Capote
Northern Plains, 1850's.
Leather with strouding trim, 42 in.
The cut of this garment is transitional between the European cut (#279) and the square cut based on earlier native garments (#286).
Denver Art Museum LPiC-1

288
Gloves
Plateau, 1880's.
Beaded leather with silk trim, 15 in.
A European concept and pattern — with individual fingers — combined with beadwork in Sahaptian style.
Denver Art Museum BBI-15

289
Woman's Ensemble
Tlingit, Alaska, 1890's.
Commercial dress, hat, gloves, and shoes, beaded cloth ornaments.
The beadwork features heraldic designs that identify the wearer's clan membership. These ornaments were worn in combination with the most fashionable clothing available.
Denver Art Museum BTI-23, 26, 28, 33

•pictured in catalog

291

283

284

290
Woman's Ensemble
Acoma Pueblo, New Mexico, 1890's.
Native wool dress, silk petticoat, and cotton underdress with lace.
This ensemble illustrates concessions to Victorian standards made in the Pueblo women's costume with the influx of American settlers who came in the wake of the transcontinental railroads.
Denver Art Museum RAc-13, 14, 15

•291
Woman's Ensemble
Navajo, Arizona, 1930's.
Calico skirt, velvet blouse with silver buttons.
A costume inspired by European fashions of the late 19th century. For an example of native Navajo woman's dress, see #102.
Denver Art Museum RNd-12, 14

•292
Woman's Ensemble
Chiricahua Apache, Arizona, 1948.
Calico with cloth tape trim.
The Apache equivalent of the Navajo's woman's well-known modern dress (see #291). This Apache costume is known as a "camp dress."
Denver Art Museum RAC-1, 2

•293
Shirt
Seminole, Florida, 1940.
Patchwork in cotton, 46 in.
A handsome example of Seminole patchwork at its finest. The colored bands on the yoke are a family-owned color scheme identifying the wearer's affiliations to other Seminoles.
Denver Art Museum RSe-1

•294
Woman's Ensemble
Seminole, Florida, c. 1910.
Calico and commercial cotton cloth.
The costume, with its flounced collar, full sleeves, and full skirt, is based upon late Victorian styles. Note the light application of patchwork which was just beginning to come into vogue at the time this costume was made.
Denver Art Museum RSe-20, 21

295
Woman's Ensemble
Seminole, Florida, 1949.
Cotton patchwork skirt, silk blouse with cotton trim.
The recent version of the turn-of-the-century style (#294). The skirt is completely patchwork and the flounce of the blouse has now become its most prominent feature.
Denver Art Museum RSe-6, 7

Further Reading

Boas, Franz. "Facial Paintings of the Indians of Northern British Columbia." *Memoirs of the American Museum of Natural History* 2(June, 1898).

Catlin, George. *O-Kee-Pa: A Religious Ceremony and Other Customs of the Mandans.* Edited and with an Introduction by John C. Ewers. New Haven: Yale University Press, 1967.

Curtis, Edward S. *The North American Indian.* Edited by F. W. Hodge. 20 vols. and Supplemental Folios. Norwood, Mass.: The Plimpton Press, 1907-1930.

Dockstader, Frederick J. *Indian Art in America.* Greenwich, Conn.: New York Graphic Society, 1961.

Douglas, Frederic H. "A Naskapi Painted Skin Shirt." *Denver Art Museum Material Culture Notes.* Denver: Denver Art Museum, 1969.

Driver, Harold E. *Indians of North America.* Chicago: University of Chicago Press, 1961.

Ewers, John C. *Plains Indian Painting.* Palo Alto: Stanford University Press, 1939.

Feder, Norman. *American Indian Art.* New York: Abrams, 1971.

Fundaburk, Emma Lila. *Southeastern Indians: Life Portraits.* Luverne, Alabama: By the author, 1958.

Grinnell, George B. *The Cheyenne Indians: Their History and Ways of Life.* 2 vols. New Haven: Yale University Press, 1923.

Harper, J. Russell. *Paul Kane's Frontier.* Austin: University of Texas Press, 1971.

Hatt, Gudmund. "Arctic Skin Clothing in Eurasia and America: An Ethnographical Study." Translated by Kirsten Taylor. *Arctic Anthropology* (5(1969): 3-132.

Hatt, Gudmund. "Moccasins and Their Relation to Arctic Footwear." *Memoirs of the American Anthropological Association* 3(1916): 149-250.

Kroeber, Alfred L. *Handbook of the Indians of California.* Bulletins of the Bureau of American Ethnology, no. 78 (1925).

Kurz, R. F. *Journal of Rudolph Friederich Kurz.* Translated by Myrtis Jarrell and edited by J. N. B. Hewitt. Bulletins of the Bureau of American Ethnology, no. 115 (1937).

Lorant, Stefan. *The New World.* New York: Duell, Sloane, and Pearce, 1946.

Mera, H. P. *Navajo Woven Dresses.* Laboratory of Anthropology General Series, no. 15 (1944).

Rudofsky, Bernard. *Are Clothes Modern?* New York: Museum of Modern Art, 1944.

Rudofsky, Bernard. *The Unfashionable Human Body.* Garden City, New York: Doubleday and Co., 1974.

Spier, Leslie. *Yuman Tribes of the Gila River.* Chicago: University of Chicago Press, 1933.

Teit, James A. "Tattooing and Face and Body Painting of the Thompson Indians." *45th Annual Report of the Bureau of American Ethnology.* Washington: Government Printing Office, 1930.

Underhill, Ruth M. *Red Man's America.* Chicago: University of Chicago Press, 1953.